ecco la cucina

To Antoinette,
Buon Appetito!

Gina

1/2012

Cover photo az. agr. Montestigliano
by Luciano Valentini-Fotostudio Gielle, Siena
Interior designs Gina Stipo
Graphic design Florido Communications

ISBN-13: 978-1-4243-2757-7
ISBN-10: 1-4243-2757-1

Publication #11,225
Printed in the United States of America by
G & R Publishing Company
800-383-1679
www.gandrpublishing.com

Table of Contents

Foreword 1

Introduction 5

Antipasti 14

    Crostini con fegatini di pollo Senese (chicken liver Senese style) ..15

        con fegatini di pollo, (chicken liver paté, Gina's version) 16

        con crema di dragoncello (tarragon cream) 17

        con funghi (mushroom) 17

        con salsa verde 18

        con cannellini (white beans) 19

    Bruschetta 19

    Pinzimonio 20

    Bagna Cauda 21

    Melanzane & Zucchini sotto Olio

        (eggplant & zucchini under oil) 22

    Calamari con Sugo Arrabiata (squid with spicy tomato sauce) 23

    Pastella per Friggere (batter for frying vegetables) 24

    Salvia Fritti con Acciughe (fried sage with anchovy) 25

    Fiori di Zucca Fritti (fried zucchini flowers) 26

    Fiori di Zucca con Caprino e Menta

        (zucchini flowers with goat cheese and mint) 27

    Uovo Sodo con Insalata e Salsa Verde

        (hard boiled eggs with salsa verde and salad) 28

Gnocchetti di Semola al Forno

    (semolina flour baked gnocchi) 29

Primi Piatti - Zuppa, Risotto, & Pasta

Zuppa (soups) 30

    di fagioli (cannellini bean) 31

    di vedura (vegetable) 32

        zuppa di pane e ribollita 32

    di ceci & pasta (Grandma Stipo's pasta fazool) 33

    di cipolla (onion) 34

    di carota & finocchio (carrot & fennel) 35

    di cavolfiore (cauliflower) 36

    di zucca gialla (winter squash) 37

    di castagne (chestnut) 38

    Vellutata di verdure (creamy vegetable soup) 39

    Croutons 39

Risotto Basics 40

    Risotto con carciofi (artichokes) 41

        con porcini...42

        con peperoni (bell peppers) 43

Crespelle con Prosciutto...44

    Besciamella..45

    Crespelle 46

Pasta...47

    Spaghetti con Carciofi (artichokes) 49

Sugo di Porcini..50

Sugo di Peperonata (bell pepper sauce).............................51

Ragù di Cinghiali (wild boar ragù)..................................52

Ragù Bianco di Anatra o Coniglio

    (white ragù of duck or rabbit)...............................53

Sugo di Pomodoro (simple tomato sauce)........................54

Pomodoro & Basilico fresco (fresh tomato & basil)...........54

Tagliatelle con Asparagi...55

Sugo di Noci e Panna (walnut cream sauce).....................56

Pomerola (vegetarian ragù)..57

Pomodoro e Ricotta (tomato & ricotta cheese).................58

Sugo di Zucchini (zucchini sauce)..................................59

Farfalle con Gorgonzola...60

Bucatini all'Amatriciana...61

Pasta fresca (fresh pasta)..62

Pasta ripieno (stuffed pasta)..63

Sugo di Salvia e Burro (sage & butter sauce)....................64

Sugo di Radicchio e Scamorza

    (radicchio & smoked mozzarella)..........................65

Ricotta e Erbe (ricotta & herbs).....................................66

Ricotta e Castagna (ricotta & chestnut)...........................67

Funghi e Tre Formaggi (mushroom & three cheeses)..........68

Zucca Gialla (winter squash)..69

Contorni e Vedure (side dishes & vegetables) 70

    Fagioli all'Uccelletto..72

    Carciofi con Limone (artichokes with lemon) 73

    Cipolle Agrodolce (baked onions) 74

    Patate Arrosto (roasted potatoes) 75

    Sformato (vegetable flan) 76

    Finnochio (fennel) 77

    Zucchini con Menta (with mint) 77

    Panzanella (tuscan bread salad) 78

    Insalata di Farro (spelt grain salad) 79

    Zucchini pancakes 80

    Peperonata (stewed peppers) 81

    Fagiolini con dragoncello (green beans w/ tarragon) 82

Secondi Piatti

    Grigliata (grilled meats) 83

    Pollo al Inferno (chicken from Hell!) 84

    Maiale Arrosto con Finocchio (roast pork w/ fennel) 85

    Pollo Arrosto con Erbe Toscane

                (roast chicken w/ Tuscan herbs) 86

    Coniglio Arrosto (roasted rabbit) 87

    Guanciale Brasato (braised veal cheeks) 88

    Pollo al Forno con Carciofi (baked chicken w/ artichokes) 89

    Petti di Pollo con Vino Bianco 90

    Torta Rustica (rustic vegetable tart) 91

Faroana con Vin Santo (guinea hen braised w/ Vin Santo) 92

Quaglia con Uva (quail w/ grapes) 93

Spezzatino (stew) 94

Involtini di Tacchino (rolled turkey breast) 95

Agnello Brasato con Chianti

       (braised lamb with Chianti wine) 96

Bracciola (beef or veal rolls) 97

Verdure dell'Estate con Salsiccia

       (summer vegetable stew with sausages) 98

Pollo con Olive e Pomodori

       (chicken with olives and tomatoes) 99

Dolci

Cantucci (biscotti) 100

Pere in Vino Rosso (poached pears in red wine) 101

Tiramisu 102

Salame Dolce 103

Crostata 104

Crespelle con Nutella 105

Pinolata (pine nut lemon cake) 106

Pannacotta 107

Cappuccino Pannacotta 107

Orange-Lemon Semifreddo 108

Mascarpone con Pesche (peaches w/ mascarpone cheese) 109

Cenci ("little rags") 110

Schiacciata (sweet grape bread) 111

Bread Dough 112

Pan co'Santi (All Saints bread) 113

Frittelle di San Giuseppe (St. Joseph fritters) 114

Castagnaccio 115

Bibliography, References, and Suggested Reading 117

Foreword

Italy has been a wonderful place to practice my art of cooking and delight in eating good food. The Italians have a relaxed love affair with their food and dinners tend to be long, congenial affairs showcasing a seemingly never-ending parade of dishes. The cooking of Italy isn't complicated, but it's important to have the freshest of seasonal ingredients. In true Italian fashion, everyone at table has an opinion -- about food in general and how to prepare specific dishes in particular. There is little fear of what one should or shouldn't eat and there is no national hysteria of dieting. Food is good, food is love, food will save your life. Italians save their paranoia for things like catching a cold from the evening breeze or the dampness of humidity!

I've been cooking, eating, or thinking about food ever since I can remember and my best childhood memories are all tied to food. When I was very young and just starting school, I moved with my family to Verona for several years. I still relate each Italian city we visited during that time with the food I ate there. Venice was stands of coconut and watermelon served with fresh cold water washing over them. Verona was the fried rounds of dough covered with sugar they sold in Piazza Erbe during the winter. Rome was the illicit ice cream bar I conned the guy into giving me outside of the catacombs when Dad refused to buy it because it was unpasteurized, and the shaved ham sandwiches on hard rolls eaten amidst the ruins of the Roman Forum. Milan was the scallop of butter on top of spaghetti with tomato sauce that changed the flavor so completely I was in awe. I remember the first time I ate a slice of Prosciutto di Parma...I went back for more and have continued that particular love affair throughout my life.

Eating pasta with red sauce and baked chicken with lemon for dinner every Sunday afternoon before vespers. Picking elderberry blossoms on my way home from school with the hope Mom would batter and fry them for a snack. Polenta with tomato sauce our Veronese housekeeper made for lunch. Climbing the fruit trees in the garden and sitting among the branches and leaves eating little yellow pears, ripe figs, juicy plums. All of these vivid and intense memories have brought me back to live in Italy.

Being of Italian descent, food in my family was an integral part of our lives. We had to be home for every meal, and dinnertime was spent talking over the events of the day or listening to the adults. As gourmet pioneers in the days before gourmet items were widely available in every grocery store, we struggled to stock good olive oil, Italian salami, cheeses and chocolates. These items were cherished and enjoyed with an almost religious devotion.

Visits to see my father's family in New York were an orgy of food and family, and the ritual of discussing at one meal what we would be having for the next meal continues in my family to this day. My grandmother was a wonderful cook and loved having us in the kitchen where we helped to make pasta, roll out the dough for fried pastries, or clean vegetables from her expansive garden, an oddity in the heart of Brooklyn. A day with my grandfather at Rockaway Beach on Long Island always ended with us picking mussels from the rock jetties to bring home for dinner, something I can't imagine doing in today's polluted waters. Grandma put everything from the sea in marinara sauce for the pasta: eels, squid, mussels, clams, snails. Only lobster managed to escape the marinara bath, and was instead baked whole with herbs, garlic, olive oil, and breadcrumbs and served ceremoniously on a plate of spaghetti. It was and still is my personal idea of heaven.

My mother was an excellent cook as well, highly curious about different foods and a student of health and nutrition, constantly seeking to feed her family in the healthiest way possible. Our family moved frequently throughout the US and Europe and wherever we went, Mom would be in the local market to sniff out any vegetable, fruit or local specialty unknown to her, which she then brought home to experiment with. I was exposed to any number of strange and wonderful foods and had tasted many delicacies long before they were common or fashionable or well-known on normal, middle-American tables. Having grown up on a farm, Mom always cultivated a garden, but her innate curiosity constantly led her to search out the local, uncultivated vegetation as well. Many different wild herbs and flowers found their way into our evening salads, from wild salty purslane she found on the sand dunes in Florida, to purple redbud blossoms on the neighbor's tree, dandelion greens from the backyard, and spring violets from the park or puffballs from the woods.

When I first came to the Siena area years ago, I learned a different kind of Italian cooking, one that was particularly tied to the land and the seasonal food it offered. The food is fresh and honest, like the food I grew up with.

I am fortunate to have found my life's work with this cuisine that I love, and I thank all the friends and family members who have helped me along the way, especially my mother, Rosemary, who taught me joy and curiosity in the kitchen. Special thanks also to Maria Grazia Florido for her help and generosity, and to all my students who help me to question and continue to grow.

This little book of recipes represents a simple collection of typical dishes of the Siena area as well as one or two from my family. I hope you enjoy making them as much as I've enjoyed learning and preparing them myself.

Buon Appetito!

Introduction

Since medieval times, Tuscany has been known as "the heart of Italy", both because geographically it is almost the center of the Italian peninsula, and because Florence was the heart and soul of the Italian Renaissance. It was Florence that emerged first from the Middle Ages into the Renaissance and spread its artists and learned scholars throughout the rest of Europe. The trade road from Northern Europe led directly through Tuscany, with Florence and Siena fighting bitterly for control of the commerce and pilgrims going in and out of Rome.

Viewing the landscape of Tuscany brings immediately to mind well-known visions of Italy, even for first-time visitors. Many of our visual conceptions of Italy are based on the famous paintings of Italian Renaissance painters and artists, many of whom were Tuscan: Cimabue, Giotto, Botticelli, Fra' Angelico, Fra' Filippo Lippi, Michelangelo, Leonardo da Vinci. The indelible perceptions they left us of what Italy looks like were often reproductions of their hometown landscapes throughout Tuscany.

Geographically, Tuscany varies greatly, from the flatlands of the coastal region around Grosseto, through ancient uninhabited forests dotted by medieval towers and villages north to Siena, where the terrain turns to moonscapes of grey soil dotted with farmhouses and lined with cypress trees. North towards the Arno River, the valleys become wider and more fertile and west towards Arezzo the terrain is lush farmland. North of Florence the rolling hills become Alp-like mountains with jagged edges and snowy caps, and west to the Tyrrhenian Sea the shining peaks reveal the ancient mining of white marble; and to the south, the Maremma, once mosquito-invested swampland and now fertile farmland.

Tuscany is ancient land and was known as Etruria before the Roman conquest. Most of the major towns and cities are continuations of the old Etruscan settlements, and from the individualistic Etruscans, the Tuscans inherited a sense of individuality shown in the medieval independent city-states and continued in the nine provinces of modern day. From north to south these are: Massa-Carrara, Pisa, Livorno, Lucca, Pistoia, Florence, Arezzo, Siena, and Grosseto.

While Florence was the heart of Renaissance art and the Medici dynasty, Siena was a medieval powerhouse in its own right. The Sienese architecture presents a preserved jewel of a medieval city. The oldest continually-operating bank in the world is Monte dei Paschi di Siena and is a modern dynasty in Tuscany, continually funding the many cultural activities and sporting events this area offers.

There is much to say about Tuscan food in general, and although much has already been written, the area around Siena deserves a special look because of the time-honored ways the Sienese people have held to their traditions. Change comes slowly, if at all, in this area, and these people continue to relate to their land, crops, and foods in much the same way their ancestors did.

The area around Siena is mainly comprised of beautiful countryside, rolling hills of sunflowers and wheat fields, acres of uninhabited wooded mountains, and simple, often isolated rural villages, connected by miles of pale dirt roads shining in the sun and winding through fields, vineyards and olive groves. Until fairly recently a rather poor agricultural region that was changed only with the new influx of tourism and industry, Tuscany's cuisine has always reflected the inherent frugality of its inhabitants and is known as "cucina povera", or poor kitchen. In medieval times, frugality and austerity were considered virtues and were both encouraged from the pulpits of the Church and occasionally legally enforced. This frugality can easily be seen in the simple austerity of the cooking of this region.

It is possible to spend a fortune in Michelin-starred restaurants that feature exotic ingredients like foie gras, ginger and lemongrass married to traditional Italian foods, and washed down with expensive Super Tuscan wines, a phrase coined for the American market. But more authentic Tuscan fare is found in the thousands of simple and elegant trattorias and osterias of the small villages and towns. These family-run affairs offer wonderful rustic dishes such as homemade pasta with a ragù of wild boar or wild hare, meats roasted or grilled over open wood fires, vegetables fresh from the family garden, and simple desserts of cantucci or crostata accompanied by Vin Santo, the Tuscan dessert wine. Brilliant, inexpensive wines from local wine producers, as well as a wide assortment of wines from all over Tuscany and Italy are generally available and very affordable.

Vegetables play an important part in the Italian diet and almost everyone has a small plot of land somewhere near their home in which to grow them. Houses seldom have grassy lawns, but instead every available inch is dedicated to the *orto*, the vegetable garden filled with rows of lettuces, artichokes, beans, winter greens, tomatoes, small fruit trees and perennial banks of rosemary, sage, and lavender surrounding all. At the edges of towns and cities are small plots of land and tool sheds rented by the apartment dwellers for the same use. With the increase of supermarkets and year-round produce availability, it is possible to get many fruits or vegetables at any time of year; but most Sienese continue the tradition of eating with the seasons. Tomatoes, peppers, zucchini and eggplants are abundant and cheap in the summer and are eaten fresh, or canned for the coming winter months. In the fall and winter, squash, cabbages, chestnuts, fennel and dark greens such as kale and rapini come into season and the menu changes accordingly. Artichokes, strawberries, asparagus, peas and fava beans are greeted enthusiastically in the spring and welcome the promise of warmer weather. At any time of year, the salads are fresh and filled with rucola, radicchio and baby lettuce dressed simply with local extra virgin olive oil.

Mushroom hunting in the late summer and fall is done in mythic proportions in the wooded hills of the Montagnola south of Siena. The people who have grown up in the rural areas know exactly what they are looking for and where to find it. Because mushrooms grow in the same spot year after year from underground spores, each person has his or her own jealously guarded spot for finding the best porcini or chanterelles. Mushroom hunting can be a clandestine affair and no one is above hiding behind a tree from another person spotted in the vicinity, be it friend, neighbor or spouse, so their most prized hunting area won't be discovered. The mushrooms find their way to the table in a myriad of dishes: creamy soups, rich pasta sauces, deep-fried in a light batter, or my favorite, simply sautéed with olive oil, garlic, and parsley. Basta, buona notte. It's delicious!

Because porcini mushrooms cannot be cultivated, they must be picked in the wild and eaten fresh during their season from late summer through the fall. They are an incredible seasonal delight. Porcini dry well and are abundant year-round in specialty stores and supermarkets at relatively inexpensive prices. Once reconstituted in fresh water, dried porcini make wonderful soups and sauces.

"A loaf of bread, a jug of wine, and thou". Most people who visit Tuscany are blown away by the wines, but fiercely disappointed by the bread. (I can't speak for the "thou" they might be travelling with.) Expecting perhaps luscious French baguettes with lots of butter or plates of olive oil for dipping, what they find are hard slices or loaves of dense, saltless bread accompanied by...nothing. There are a number of stories as to "why" the Tuscan bread is saltless. Because salt was taxed, the austere Tuscans considered it too expensive to use with abandon and so they began leaving the salt out of the bread so they could afford it to cure their salami and prosciutto. As well, in the small towns and villages there often was only one oven shared by the townspeople, and each family had their own day once a week to bake the family bread. By the end of the week, the leftover bread became stale. Because the bread has no salt, it doesn't attract moisture from the air and therefore doesn't mold. The bread can be kept for weeks and will just get harder and denser, but still remain edible. Due to the inherent frugality of the Tuscan people, an entire cuisine has developed based on making use of leftover bread. It is added to soups, which the Sienese like very thick, and makes a wonderful summer salad, called *panzanella*. But whatever the reason, the simple fact is that the bread is an excellent foil and accompaniment to the intensely flavored foods and salty cured meats the Tuscans love.

Historically, the available grazing land around Siena was used for sheep instead of cattle, with the exception of the Chianina cows raised around Arezzo. These cows are renowned for their lean and tender meat and are a necessity for the popular *bistecca di fiorentina*. This T-bone cut, cooked over hot coals from a wood fire and served rare, originated in Florence but is now available in all of Tuscany. The abundance of olive trees and sheep produced a cuisine relying heavily on olive oil, with the cheeses of this area being made from sheeps' milk, the famous *pecorino* for which the zone around Pienza to the south is especially known.

The Sienese diet heavily favors pork, along with lamb, chicken and rabbit. The vast number of pigs raised, especially the recently revived species known as *cinta senese,* ensures excellent fresh pork dishes such as *porchetta,* (whole de-boned roasted pig), and pork roasts, as well as a wide range of salami and prosciutto. *Lardo di Colonnata* is wonderfully sweet cured pork fat from Massa-Carrara, and *fiocchiona* is a special salami made with wild fennel seeds. If you find yourself here in the winter, look for roasted pancetta, which is a roll of uncured bacon rubbed with the traditional sage and rosemary and roasted in the oven. It's fatter than a normal pork roast but it's really too delicious to miss.

Wild game is another integral part of the Tuscan diet, and with so much uninhabited land the wild game abounds. Pheasant, quail, hare and deer can be frequently seen as you drive through the country, and I've often encountered wild boar on isolated roads and picked up porcupine quills on my walks in the woods. Even though porcupine is illegal to hunt or kill, even accidentally, the people living in the hills make a wonderful stew with it. I call it Tuscan possum!

Fresh herbs are widely cultivated and used in this region, for both medicinal uses and in cooking. Wild rosemary, fennel, sage, mint and thyme grow in abundance and are also cultivated in the home gardens. There are a number of wild herbs and lettuces that are picked in the spring and added to pasta, risotto or soup. Tarragon *(dragoncello)*, has been used in Siena for hundreds of years, the only region of Italy to make use of it.

The wooded hills around Siena are filled with chestnut trees and harvested in the fall. They are eaten boiled with fennel seeds or roasted over open wood fires. The spicey, meaty nuts are also dried or made into flour for *castagnaccia*, a traditional Tuscan dessert of chestnut gruel spread thin and baked with olive oil, rosemary and raisins.

For the wine lover, Siena has much to offer. Because it is in the heart of Tuscany's best wine production area, it's an excellent staging point for wine tours. The wine communities of Chianti and San Gimignano are to the north and west, with those of Montalcino and Montepulciano to the south. The newly discovered wines of the Maremma and Bolgheri are an easy drive away. The national wine institute of Italy, Enoteca Italiana, is located in the fortress of Siena and offers a vast collection of hundreds of wines from all over Italy, with a wine bar for tasting.

The recipes included in this book are a compilation of what I've learned from the chefs, restaurateurs, and home cooks I've worked with and had the pleasure of sharing a dinner or two. The Sienese are a generous people and are always willing to discuss their passion for food over a shared meal. The most we can do is delve into the accompanying recipes and do our best to replicate the wonderful dishes served and enjoyed in this region.

Antipasti

Most Tuscans start their dinner with a simple antipasto, which means a snack before the meal. The most common of these are *affettati misti*, or sliced cured meats like prosciutto and salami; *crostini*, sliced baquettes with cold or warm toppings; *bruschetta* (pronounced broos-ketta) which is toasted bread topped with extra virgin olive or chopped tomatoes; or a wide variety of little salads, pickled vegetables, or simple dishes to whet your appetite. At formal dinners the antipasti can be quite extensive and varied. Following are a few of my favourite dishes.

Crostini

The most popular of *Sienese* antipasti, *crostini* are untoasted slices of bread topped with a variety of spreads, either cold or warm. No serious dinner is complete without a platter of assorted *crostini* and the people here have an undying enthusiasm for eating them.

Crostini con i Fegatini di Pollo (chicken livers)

This is a traditional recipe from Siena for crostini topped with chicken livers.

> 1/2 lb chicken livers, cleaned
> 1/2 onion, chopped
> 4 tbsp olive oil
> 1/2 cup white wine
> 1 teas capers
> 1 teas anchovies
> 2 sage leaves
> salt

Sauté the onion in the olive oil until soft, add the chicken livers, salt and sage and sauté 15 minutes. Add the white wine and allow it to cook off. Add the capers and anchovies to the chicken livers and pass it through a food mill, or chop finely by hand. Spread on slices of bread and serve.

Paté di Fegatini alla Gina (chicken liver paté)

I readily admit that over the years my method of making Tuscan chicken livers for crostini morphed into more of a French paté by the addition of more butter and cream. Using a sweet wine such as Vin Santo, Monbazillac or Reisling, smooths out the flavours and is richer than what would normally be found in this area, but I prefer this to the traditional Sienese recipe.

1/2 lb chicken livers, cleaned
1 tbsp olive oil
3 tbsp butter
2 shallots or 1 small onion, chopped
2 sage leaves
1/2 cup Vin Santo, or a sweet white or dessert wine
salt & pepper
2-3 tbsp cream

Sauté the shallots in the olive oil and 2 tbsp butter until transparent, add the livers and sage and continue to cook until the livers are cooked, being careful not to brown them. Add the Vin Santo, salt & pepper to taste, and allow the wine to cook off. Add the cream and cook 1 minute, remove from heat. Add the remaining 1 tbsp butter and puree in a food processor until smooth. Allow to cool slightly and serve warm or cold on sliced baquettes.

Crostini con Crema di Dragoncello (tarragon cream)

>1 cup ricotta or fresh farmers cheese
>2 tbsp fresh tarragon
>1 small garlic clove, chopped
>salt & pepper

Combine all in a food processor and puree till smooth, adding additional milk or cream if too thick.

Crostini con Funghi (mushrooms)

>1/2 lb mushrooms, finely chopped
>1/4 cup dry porcini, soaked in water and chopped
>1/2 teas fresh rosemary, finely chopped
>2 garlic cloves, minced
>olive oil
>1/4 cup white wine
>salt & pepper

In a sauté pan, gently cook the garlic in olive oil, add the mushrooms, porcini and rosemary. Sauté over medium heat until well cooked, add the soaking water from the porcini, the wine, salt & pepper to taste and continue to cook until the liquid cooks off. Top the crostini with the mixture and serve.

Crostini con Salsa Verde

This bright sauce is used in a variety of ways. Traditionally served with boiled chicken and beef, it is also wonderful as an antipasto spread on crostini or can be used to top hard-boiled eggs.

1 large bunch Italian parsley, stems included
1 bunch arugula
1 teas anchovy paste
1 teas capers
1 hard boiled egg
2 garlic cloves
1 tbsp mayonnaise
salt & pepper
olive oil

Combine all in a food processor and puree until smooth, adding olive oil if the mixture is too thick. As the anchovies are salty, you'll need to check for salt before adding any.

Crostini con Crema di Cannellini
(white bean puree)

 2 cups cooked cannellini beans
 2 garlic cloves, chopped
 1 teas fresh rosemary
 3 sage leaves
 salt & pepper
 olive oil

Sauté the garlic in a small amount of olive oil until soft, add the rosemary, sage and the cannellini beans. Allow them to heat through, salt & pepper to taste, remove from the heat and allow to cool slightly. Puree in a food processor, adding olive oil to make a smooth, spreadable cream. Check for salt and spread on crostini.

Bruschetta

Also known in Tuscany as "fettunta", bruschetta is made by toasting slices of bread over an open fire on a grate, rubbing the slices very lightly with a fresh garlic clove and then drizzling them with good extra virgin olive oil. (A little garlic goes a long way, be careful or all you will taste is raw garlic.) It's wonderful just like this and is the traditional vehicle for tasting the new olive oil in the fall. The slices can also be topped with a mixture of fresh tomatoes, basil, salt and pepper, or Lardo di Colonnata. Lardo is the cured fat from the belly of the pig, seasoned with rosemary and salt, and is luxurious as it warms up and becomes translucent on the warm toast.

Pinzimonio

Pinzimonio is the Tuscan equivalent of French *crudités*, simple to make and a refreshing starter to any meal, but especially good when the vegetables are at their freshest or the extra virgin olive oil is newly pressed. The fresh vegetables are served together on a large platter and each person is given a small, individual bowl of quality extra-virgin olive oil, into which has been put a good quantity of salt and a generous grinding of black pepper. The veggies are then dipped into the olive oil and eaten at leisure and at the table, with lots of good wine and conversation.

Cut or slice a variety of fresh vegetables, such as red peppers, carrots, celery, fennel, scallions, cherry tomatoes, zucchini, cucumbers, radishes, baby artichokes, tiny baby lettuce heads, etc. Try for an interesting variety of colors, placing them on a large platter in the middle of the table for your guests to help themselves.

Bagna Cauda

In the northern region of Piedmonte, they have a dish similar to *pinzimonio* called *bagna cauda*, or "warm bath". Consisting of equal parts of olive oil and butter and generous amounts of finely chopped garlic and minced anchovy fillets, it is a welcome starter on a cold wintry evening. It is served in the same way as *pinzimonio*, although they have special bowls in Piedmonte for the *bagna cauda*, with space under the bowl for a votive candle to keep the oil hot.

    1 stick butter
    1/2 cup good extra-virgin olive oil
    4 garlic cloves, minced
    4 anchovy fillets, minced

Place all ingredients in a pan over a medium fire and bring to a simmer. Allow to sit 10 minutes or more, reheat and serve.

Melanzane & Zucchini sott' Olio
(grilled eggplant and zucchini)

This is a wonderful summer addition to an antipasto platter and easy to do if the barbeque grill is already fired up. The vegetables can be either grilled over the coals or roasted on a high heat on a rack in the oven.

zucchini
eggplant
parsley, coarsely chopped
garlic cloves, cleaned and slivered
salt
extra virgin olive oil

Wash and slice the vegetables lengthwise. Place them, unadorned, on the grill and cook until they soften and develop grill marks, or lay them on a rack in a hot oven, 450°, until they are slightly toasted and soft. There should be some nice grill marks in the oven as well, but it's not critical to the dish.

Layer the vegetables while still hot in a high sided, narrow dish, and sprinkle with salt, garlic and parsley, continuing to layer until all the vegetables are finished. Cover with olive oil and allow to sit for 30 minutes to an hour. Remove the vegetables from the oil and serve. The oil can be saved for another use, perhaps to dress the salad or other vegetables.

Calamari con Sugo Arrabiata
(squid with spicy tomato sauce)

This recipe frequently uses *moscardine*, tiny octopuses, which may be found in specialty fish departments. You can also substitute *calamari*, or squid. To remain tender and not rubbery, squid should either be cooked very quickly or, as in this recipe, cooked for a long time.

> 1/2 lb squid, caps and tentacles
> 3 garlic cloves
> olive oil
> hot peppers, one or two
> 1 cup tomato sauce
> parsley
> white wine

Cut the squid caps into rings. Sauté the garlic in the olive oil gently, add the hot peppers and parsley and cook a few minutes, then add squid and sauté until cooked through. Add the wine, allow it to cook off and then add the tomato and simmer for 30 minutes, salting to taste. Serve as an antipasto with bread for dipping.

Pastella per friggere
(batter for frying vegetables or shrimp)

This simple tempura-like batter is wonderful for dipping sage leaves, zucchini flowers, cauliflower, mushrooms, fresh porcini, zucchini slices, shrimp or fish. (Use tiny shrimp and leave the edible shells on, they fry up to a nice crunch.) You don't measure the ingredients as you make however much you think you will need. Substituting beer for the wine is nice when frying fish.

> flour
> white wine (or beer)
> salt
> oil for frying

Put enough flour in a bowl to make the appropriate amount of batter for what you intend to fry. Add salt, a teaspoon for 2 cups of flour, and with a whisk begin adding the wine or beer slowly, whisking and pouring simultaneously and constantly, until the mixture is the consistency of a thin pancake batter. Allow to sit for a few minutes before using, whisk again and dip each piece in the batter before frying in hot oil.

Salvia Fritto con Acciughe
(fried sage with anchovy)

Sage grows in abundance all year long and is widely used in Tuscan cooking. Combined with anchovy, dipped in a light batter and fried, it also makes a delicious appetizer to be enjoyed with a cold glass of white wine.

> batter for frying
> sage leaves (several per person)
> anchovy paste

Take a sage leaf and with your finger spread a small "shmear" of anchovy paste on one side of the leaf. Press together with another sage leaf to form a sandwich. Make a plate of these and prepare the paper towels for draining the fried leaves.

In a high-sided skillet put peanut or sunflower oil to the depth of 1 inch and heat. When the oil is hot enough to immediately fry a small amount of batter, dip the sage leaves into the batter and fry them in the oil, turning them over as they brown. Don't add too many at one time, as crowding the pan reduces the temperature of the oil and creates steam, resulting in a finished product which is oily and less crunchy. As they turn golden brown, take them out and drain them on the paper towels. Just the single leaves, without the anchovy sandwich, are delicious as well.

Fiori di Zucca Fritti (fried zucchini flowers)

Zucchini flowers are wonderful fried and can be stuffed with sage and chopped fresh pecorino for a delightful Tuscan flavour. If you don't wish to stuff them, just clean them and dip them in the batter and fry.

zucchini flowers, cleaned 2-3 per person
fresh sage leaves, chopped
fresh pecorino cheese, small dice
batter for frying
oil for frying

Clean the zucchini flowers by removing the spikes on the outside at the bottom of the flower and the stamen inside. It's best done when the flowers are open in the morning, but if they are already closed when you get them, just be careful not to rip the flower too much. It's best not to wash the flowers, just brush them off to clean.

If you wish to stuff the flowers, mix the chopped sage and pecorino together in a small bowl and place a teaspoon of the mixture into the flower. When the olive oil is hot, dip each flower into the batter and fry until golden brown, turning once. Drain on paper towels and serve.

Fiore di Zucca con Caprino e Menta
(zucchini flowers w/ goat cheese & mint)

zucchini blossoms, 2-3 per person
goat cheese
mint leaves, chopped
cherry tomatoes, quartered
olive oil
salt

Clean the blossoms by removing the stamen inside and the long spikes at the base of the flower. Mix softened goat cheese with mint leaves and a little salt and carefully stuff the blossoms, being careful not to tear the leaves. Place them in an oiled baking dish big enough to accommodate all of them in one layer, top with tomatoes, drizzle with olive oil and a sprinkling of salt, and bake for 10 minutes in the oven at 375° until the goat cheese is warmed through. Serve as an antipasto or as a side dish.

Uovo Sodo con Insalata e Salsa Verde
(hard boiled eggs with salad & salsa verde)

A lovely fresh start to any spring or summer menu.

hard boiled eggs, one per person
salsa verde (page 18)
mixed baby lettuces
1 tbsp balsamic vinegar
3 tbsp olive oil
salt

Mix the vinegar, olive oil and salt together to make a simple vinaigrette and toss a small amount with the lettuce leaves. Place them in the middle of a plate, peel and cut the eggs in half, arranging them on the lettuce. Top the eggs with the salsa verde and serve.

Gnocchetti di Semola al Forno
(baked semolina gnocchi)

My sister, Mary, first tasted this at a dinner in my contrada, the Selva. She loved it so much she begged me to get the recipe from Valeria, the cook who is from northern Italy. It's a polenta-like starter which is also great served as a side with stews and braised dishes.

> 1 quart milk
> 1 1/2 cups semolina flour
> 1 stick butter
> 2 egg yolks
> grated parmigiano or grana padana
> sage leaves
> salt

Bring milk and 1 teaspoon salt to a boil, reduce to a simmer and whisking vigorously, very gradually add the semolina flour, picking up the flour a little at a time with your hand and allowing the grains to fall through your fingers.

Take off the fire, add the butter and egg yolks and spread onto a buttered baking dish. Dot with more butter, spread generously with parmigiano and sage leaves and bake in a 375° oven until golden brown. Serve warm or room temperature.

Primi Piatti

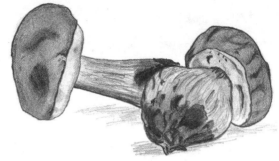

The *primo piatto*, or first course, is generally where the Italians consume the starch of their meal and consists of either a pasta, risotto, or soup. At an important dinner or special occasion, it is not uncommon to serve two or three first courses. Pasta and risotto are never eaten with the meat course, but are always consumed by themselves beforehand, while soups are the staff of life and often are a meal unto themselves, followed only by a cheese course.

Zuppa

Soups are a hearty addition to the fall and winter table and in Siena and the surrounding area are typically very dense and thick, almost like a stew. Pasta is often added and cooked directly in the finished soup. Frequently stale bread is added, both as a way of using up the bread and as a method of thickening the soup. Tuscans like their soups stick-to-the-ribs thick, but most of these recipes have been thinned down a bit. It's simply a matter of how much broth is used at the end and how much bread is added to the bowl.

Zuppa di Fagioli (cannellini bean soup)

This is one of the most common soups eaten in this area and is made with either white cannellini beans or ceci (chick peas). Pasta or bread is frequently used to thicken the soup to a stew-like consistency and in the fall and winter, new olive oil is drizzled on top before serving.

4 cups cannellini beans, soaked 4 hours
1 bay leaf
1 onion, chopped
1/4 cup olive oil
1 quart chicken or vegetable stock
1/2 cup tomato puree
1/2 teas fresh rosemary, chopped
salt and pepper
pasta, small shapes for soup

Pour soaking liquid off beans, add fresh water and simmer until beans are cooked through, adding 2 teas of salt and a bay leaf halfway through. Remove any foam that forms on the top as the beans cook.

Sauté the onions in olive oil until soft. Add fresh rosemary and sauté gently 5 minutes. Add beans, tomato and chicken broth and cook at least 30 minutes. Puree the beans with an immersion blender or food mill, return to the heat, adding additional water or stock if too thick. Salt and pepper to taste.

Bring soup to a boil, add pasta and cook until done. Or you can cook the pasta separately in boiling water, drain it and add it to the soup. Serve with parmigiano and a drizzle of olive oil.

Zuppa di Verdura (vegetable soup)

1 onion, chopped
2 celery stalks, chopped
3 carrots, peeled and chopped
1 cup cabbage, chopped
2 potatoes, peeled and chopped
2 cups swiss chard or kale, chopped
1/2 cup olive oil
1 cup cannellini beans
1 cup tomatoes, chopped
2 tbsp each fresh parsley and basil, chopped
rind from parmigiano, optional
salt and pepper

Sauté the onions, carrots and celery in the olive oil in a large soup pot, about 10 minutes. Add the cabbage, kale and potatoes and stir to coat with oil. Add the beans, tomatoes and herbs along with several quarts of fresh water, 2 times the amount of veggies. Add the parmigiano rind and cook slowly several hours, until beans are cooked. Season with salt and pepper while cooking. Remove the cheese rind, but don't throw it away, it's delicious right out of the pot! If desired, small soup pasta can be added and cooked right in the soup. Serve over a slice of stale bread and a sprinkling of parmigiano.

Zuppa di Pane is a Tuscan recipe using this soup and lots of bread layered in a soup tureen. Ribollita is a traditional soup, meaning literally "reboiled", and is the preceding soup made with lots of bread and left to be reheated the next day. While the cannellini beans and winter greens are optional in a vegetable soup, they are key ingredients in a good ribollita.

Zuppa di Ceci e Pasta
(Grandma Stipo's pasta fazool)

This quick and easy soup from the Campania region is brothy and filled with whole ceci, herbs and pasta.

> 1 can ceci, or two cups cooked ceci (aka chick peas
>   or garbanzo beans)
> 3 garlic cloves, chopped
> olive oil
> 1 tbsp each fresh parsley and basil, chopped
> hot pepper flakes
> salt
> cooked pasta, elbow or other small shape

Sauté the garlic in the oil, being careful not to brown. Add pepper flakes to your liking, hot or mild. Add the ceci beans, fresh herbs and two cans or 3 cups water, and salt to taste. Allow to simmer gently about 10 minutes. Add cooked pasta before serving and top with a generous grating of parmigiano.

Zuppa di Cipolle (onion soup)

8 large onions, peeled, quartered, and sliced thin
2 tbsp butter
1/2 cup olive oil
3 quarts chicken or beef stock
1/4 cup cream (optional)
1/4 parmigiano, grated
Italian or French bread slices
gruyere cheese

Melt the butter and olive oil in a heavy soup pot, add the onions and sauté slowly until translucent, at least 30 minutes. Add the heated broth to the onions and allow to simmer 1 hour. Mix together the cream and parmigiano, whisk into the soup and simmer 2 minutes. Toast bread slices in oven until dry, top with slices of cheese and place in bottom of soup bowls. Ladle the hot soup over the bread and serve immediately.

Zuppa di Carota e Finocchio
(carrot & fennel soup)

    1 lb carrots, cleaned and chopped
    1 lb fresh fennel, chopped
    1 onion, chopped
    olive oil
    3 cups chicken or vegetable broth or water
    salt
    white pepper

Sauté the onion in olive oil until soft. Add carrots and fennel and continue to cook over a medium heat, covered, until the veggies are very soft, at least 30 minutes, adding a small amount of water or broth to prevent the bottom from sticking or burning. Add salt while cooking. Remove from heat, add broth and puree with an immersion blender until smooth. The consistency should be of a thick soup, you may add additional broth if you deem it to be too thick. Before serving, reheat and stir in a light grinding of white pepper. May be topped with chopped fennel fronds and croutons.

Zuppa di Cavolfiore (Cauliflower Soup)

A wonderful hearty winter soup, it is slightly pureed with chunks of vegetable and scented with fresh rosemary.

1 head cauliflower, chopped
1 small onion, chopped
2 cloves garlic, chopped
olive oil
1 teas fresh rosemary
3 cups chicken or vegetable broth or water
salt
white pepper

Sauté the onion and garlic in olive oil until soft, add fresh rosemary and cook 2 minutes, add cauliflower and stir to coat with the oil. Add 2 cups of broth or water and salt & pepper and allow to simmer until cauliflower is soft. Remove from heat and puree with an immersion blender just until the soup thickens, with chunks of vegetable remaining, adding the additional broth as needed to form a thick soup. Before serving, return to heat. Serve topped with croutons or a drizzle of good olive oil.

Zuppa di Zucca Gialla (Winter squash soup)

An elegant, velvety soup, simple to make and a colorful start to a fall or winter menu.

    2 medium onions, chopped
    4 tbsp butter and olive oil, combined
    8 cups butternut, acorn or pumpkin
    6 cups broth
    1/2 - 1 cup cream
    grating of fresh nutmeg, 1/2 tsp
    salt and pepper
    croutons
    chopped chives

Split the squash in half, coat the cut ends with olive oil, and roast the in the oven until soft. Remove from oven and when cool, scoop squash into a bowl. Sauté onion in butter and oil until soft and translucent, add roasted squash and sauté for a few minutes to coat with oil. Add a small amount of broth and continue to cook to meld flavours for at least 30 minutes, adding broth or water as necessary to keep it from sticking or burning. Salt to taste and add nutmeg.

Puree the mixture using an immersion blender. Return to the heat, adding enough broth or water to form a thick soup and cook for 10 minutes.

Stir the cream into the soup. Keep soup hot but do not allow it to boil. Serve soup topped with croutons and chopped chives or toasted pumpkin seeds. Or place a spoonful of sauteed porcini mushrooms in the middle of the soup for a truly luxurious first course.

Zuppa di Castagna (chestnut soup)

The wooded hills south of Siena are filled with chestnut trees and harvested in the fall. They are eaten boiled with fennel seeds or roasted over open wood fires. This soup is a wonderful winter dish made with boiled chestnuts, rosemary and pancetta. Either fresh or dried chestnuts can be used and the pancetta can be omitted for a vegetarian dish.

4 oz pancetta, chopped
1 small onion, chopped
1 leek, chopped
1/4 bulb fresh fennel, chopped
1 garlic clove, minced
2 tbsp olive oil
4 tbsp butter
1 sprig rosemary, chopped
4 cups chestnuts
water
salt
2 bay leaves
1/2 cup cream

Boil the fresh chestnuts in enough water to cover for 20 minutes. Peel the chestnuts, taking them from the pot of water one at a time. If they are at all difficult to peel, put them back in the water or reheat the water. Chestnuts peel easiest when very hot. If using dried chestnuts, soak them in water until softened, 1-2 hours.

Sauté the pancetta in a soup pot, remove to the side when lightly browned. Add the butter and olive oil to the pan and sauté the onion, leek, garlic and fennel until soft and translucent. Add the rosemary, then the pancetta and boiled chestnuts. Stir to coat with the oil, add enough water to the pan to cover, add the bay leaves, salt to taste and simmer for 30 minutes. Just before serving add the cream. Serve with croutons.

Vellutata di Verdure

This basic recipe for a creamy vegetable soup, known as a vellutata, can be made with a variety of vegetables. Fresh asparagus or pea is lovely in the spring, in the winter try broccoli or leek.

> 1 lb vegetable, chopped (broccoli, asparagus, peas or leeks)
> 1 small onion, chopped
> olive oil
> 3 cups chicken or vegetable broth
> 1/4 cup cream
> salt
> white pepper

Sauté the onion in olive oil until soft, add vegetable and continue to cook over a medium heat until the vegetable is coated with the oil and begins to cook, then add 1/2 cup of broth or water and salt & pepper. When the vegetable is cooked, add broth to cover and cook 15 more minutes, remove from heat and puree with an immersion blender until smooth. The consistency should be thick, add more liquid if necessary. Before serving, return to heat and add cream if desired. Serve topped with croutons or a drizzle of good olive oil.

Croutons: decrust and cube a loaf of bread, place the cubes in a baking dish, drizzle with extra virgin olive oil and salt and bake at 400° until golden, stirring occasionally.

Risotto

Although risotto originated as a staple of northern Italian cooking in the regions of Lombardy, Piedmont, and the Veneto, its creaminess and diversity have found it a home on tables throughout Italy. A wide variety of vegetables can be used, changing with the seasons and with what is fresh and in abundance. The dish can be finished with any combination of cream, butter and parmigiano, and adjusted to the preference of the cook. I, for instance, tend to use all three!

Once you understand the principles of making risotto, you can add any variety of ingredients you like without compromising the finished product, which should be full of flavor and creamy, rolling off the spoon. The basic rules that should be followed to ensure a successful risotto are these:

* always use a short-grain Italian rice such as arborio or carnaroli; these grains have layers of starch that, when stirred continually in hot liquid, shed to form the characteristic creaminess of the dish.
* make a *sofritto* by sautéing first the onion or garlic, then the vegetable, in olive oil, then add the rice, coating and heating the grains with the hot oil.
*add wine and allow it to cook off before adding the hot stock; use a good quality broth rather than water for more flavor and add it a small amount at a time, stirring constantly to help the grains shed their starch.
*don't overcook the rice, it should be *al dente*, which means you should feel the kernels on your tooth when you bite into it.
*your guests should be seated and ready to eat as risotto doesn't fair well if left to sit and wait on the guests.

The following recipe can be used as a basic guideline and I've included some suggestions for variations.

Risotto con Carciofi (artichokes)

> 3 cloves garlic, chopped
> 1/4 cup olive oil
> 2 tbsp butter
> 2 cups chopped fresh artichokes
> 1 cup white wine
> 2 cups arborio or carnaroli rice
> 6-8 cups chicken or vegetable stock
> 1/4 cup butter
> 2 tbsp parsley, chopped
> 1/4 cup parmigiano

Heat the broth to almost boiling and keep hot. In a large pot, sauté the garlic in olive oil, add the butter and the artichokes and sauté until soft, about 10 minutes.

Add the rice and stir to coat with oil. Add the white wine, stirring until absorbed. Add the broth one cup at a time, stirring until the liquid is absorbed with each addition. Continue this process until the rice is cooked, with the interior of the kernels being *al dente*. Check for salt.

Stir in the butter, parsley, and parmigiano. The risotto will stiffen quickly, so serve it immediately, adding additional liquid as needed right before serving to maintain the characteristic creaminess of the dish.

Risotto con Porcini

This risotto can also be made with wild mushrooms by substituting one cup of fresh wild mushrooms (chanterelles, shitake, black trumpets, etc.) for half the dried porcini.

> 3 cloves garlic, chopped
> 1/4 cup olive oil
> 1 cup dried porcini, soaked in water till soft
> 1/2 teas fresh chopped rosemary
> 1 cup white wine
> 2 cups arborio or carnaroli rice
> 6-8 cups chicken or vegetable stock
> 2 tbsp parsley, chopped
> 1/4 cup cream
> 1/4 cup parmigiano

Heat the broth to almost boiling and keep hot. In a large pot sauté the garlic in olive oil, add the chopped porcini and rosemary and sauté until soft, about 5 minutes.

Add the rice and stir to coat with oil. Add the white wine, stirring until absorbed. Add the water used to soak the porcini and stir, add the broth one cup at a time, stirring until the liquid is absorbed with each addition. Continue this process until the rice is cooked, with the interior of the kernels being *al dente*. Check for salt.

Stir in the cream, parsley, and parmigiano. The risotto will stiffen quickly, so serve it immediately, adding additional liquid as needed right before serving to maintain the characteristic creaminess of the dish.

Risotto con Peperoni (bell peppers)

In the summertime when peppers are in season and fresh from the garden, this is a lovely side dish to roasted chicken.

3 cloves garlic, chopped
1/4 cup olive oil
2 bell peppers, red or yellow
1 cup white wine
2 cups arborio or carnaroli rice
6-8 cups chicken or vegetable stock
2 tbsp butter
1/4 cup cream
2 tbsp parsley, chopped
1/4 cup parmigiano

Heat the broth to almost boiling and keep hot. In a large pot sauté the garlic in olive oil, add the chopped peppers and sauté until soft, about 10 minutes.

Add the rice and stir to coat with oil. Add the white wine, stirring until absorbed. Add the broth one cup at a time, stirring until the liquid is absorbed with each addition. Continue this process until the rice is cooked, with the interior of the kernels being *al dente*. Check for salt.

Stir in the butter, cream, parsley, and parmigiano. The risotto will stiffen quickly, so serve it immediately, adding additional liquid as needed right before serving to maintain the characteristic creaminess of the dish.

Baked Crespelle conProsciutto

Crespelle, or crepes, are a popular first course, rolled and baked in the oven with besciamella sauce. Make the crespelle ahead of time, they will keep covered with plastic wrap for a several days in the fridge.

crespelle, two per person
sautéed spinach, drained
sautéed mushrooms, drained
besciamella sauce
prosciutto, thinly sliced
parmigiano, grated

Place a crepe on your work surface and top with a slice of prosciutto, a small amount of spinach and mushrooms and a sprinkle of parmigiano. Roll up, leaving sides open, and place side by side in a baking dish, the bottom of which you've spread with a thin layer of besciamella sauce. Top with besciamella and parmigiano and bake at 350° until browned, about 30 minutes. With a spatula, carefully remove from the baking pan to individual plates, one or two per person.

Besciamella

> 4 tbsp butter
> 4 tbsp flour
> 4 cups milk, heated
> 1 teas salt
> 1/2 teas pepper
> 1/2 teas ground nutmeg

Melt butter on a medium heat, add the flour, stirring constantly until flour is absorbed. This forms a roux and should be allowed to gently cook for a few minutes to allow the flour taste to be cooked out. Be very careful not to brown the roux.

Stir in the hot milk slowly, whisking vigorously to avoid lumps. Add salt, pepper, and nutmeg and continue to simmer over medium heat for 15 minutes. Taste to correct seasonings.

Crespelle (crepes)

Crepes are originally from Italy and were most likely introduced to the French by Catherine d'Medici in the 15th century.

2 cups flour
4 eggs, beaten
2 tbsp melted butter
2 cups milk, more if needed
dash nutmeg
1/2 teas salt

Mix liquid ingredients together, make a well in the flour and add the liquid ingredients to the flour. Whisk together, add salt and nutmeg. Strain the crepes batter to remove any lumps.

Using a non-stick skillet or crepes pan, heat a small amount of butter or oil, add a small scoop of the batter to the heated pan, tilting and turning the pan quickly to evenly distribute the batter before it sets. The crepes should be thin and even. Turn the crepe as soon as it is cooked through and blonde, before the bottom browns excessively. Stack them on top of each other as they are done.

Pasta

Pasta is very much a mainstay of the Italian diet and can historically be indicative of the dividing line between the wealth of the north and the poverty of the south of Italy. Originally, the northern regions made their rich egg-based ribbons of tagliatelle and stuffed tortelloni and ravioli only on Sundays and holidays and relied on polenta, rice and bread for their main starch. The southern regions made their macaroni with hard durum wheat and water, but instead of special occasion food, it formed the principle starch of their diet. Today *pastasciutta*, or dried boxed pasta, is eaten in all regions of Italy and consumed at least once a day.

The history of pasta in Italy did not originate with the adventures of Marco Polo, as many have been led to believe, but was actually firmly rooted in the diet of Italians for generations before he was even born. In Naples, they had machines to extrude pasta shapes in the 1500's and there has been evidence found in Etruscan tombs that leads us to believe that the people who inhabited Tuscany before the Romans made a type of hand-rolled spaghetti. In fact, in the region of Siena and especially around Montalcino, a type of hand-rolled spaghetti, called *pici* or *pinci*, is still made today from hard winter wheat, olive oil and water. In Montalcino, it's a cottage industry, with the little old ladies making the *pici* at home in the morning and selling them to the restaurants to serve for dinner.

Italians feel so strongly about pasta's healthy, life-giving qualities that they buy specially processed 5 kilo sacks of it for their dogs and cats. Pasta is good for all!

Special attention is given to the type of pasta served and the appropriate sauce with which to marry it. As a general rule, spaghetti or linguini are used for oil-based sauces, flat-surfaced pastas such as farfalle are used for creamy sauces, and meat sauces are matched with pasta shapes that have holes and crevices for catching the bits of meat, such as penne and rigatoni. The type of sauce will also determine whether you'll use a macaroni made from hard wheat flour and water or the more delicate and rich pasta made with whole eggs and soft wheat flour. Suggestions are made with the following recipes for the type of pasta to use. Ragù is generally a meat-based sauce and is most often served on tagliatelle or the wider papparadelle. The word *sugo* means "sauce" and often indicates a sauce without meat.

Pasta in Italy is eaten *al dente*, which translates literally "to the tooth" and means that they want to feel some resistance on the tooth when they eat it. When you bite into it you can see a minute amount of uncooked pasta on the very inside, which Italians say renders the pasta more digestible.

Ravioli and stuffed pasta, which originated in the north, are now found in every region of Italy. In Tuscany, these rich and elegant pastas are most often topped with a simple sauce of butter and fresh sage leaves in order not to overwhelm and mask the delicacy of the filling.

When cooking pasta, some important tips to remember:

- Don't overcook the pasta, follow the cooking time suggestions on the outside of the box.
- Fresh egg pasta should be cooked no more than 1 – 1 1/2 minutes, depending on the size.
- Never rinse pasta. To avoid the pasta sticking together after it has been drained either dress it immediately with your intended sauce or toss it with a little olive oil or butter.
- Always salt the water before cooking pasta. No matter how flavourful your sauce, if you've cooked the pasta in unsalted water it will taste lifeless.

Spaghetti con Carciofi (spaghetti w/ artichokes)

       4 artichokes, one per person
       3 garlic cloves
       extra virgin olive oil
       2 tbls butter
       1/2 cup juice from lemons and oranges
       salt
       parmigiano
       parsley

Clean artichokes, removing tough outer leaves, peeling and trimming stem; cut in half and remove any choke. Put cleaned artichokes in water with juice of a lemon to avoid them browning. Slice the artichokes when ready to cook.

Sauté garlic until softened in olive oil, add butter, olive oil and artichokes, sauté 10 minutes. Add citrus juices and salt and continue to cook 15 minutes on low heat, adding a bit of water if too dry. Add cooked spaghetti or linguini with small amount of pasta water and toss, adding additional olive oil, about 2 tablespoons, and fresh chopped parsley. Toss with parmigiano and serve.

This sauce can also be made with canned artichoke hearts without compromising the finished product.

Sugo di Porcini (porcini mushroom sauce)

While fresh porcini can be used, the dried porcini are really more adapted to this easy sauce. Sautéed Italian sausage can also be added for a meaty, hearty winter dish.

> 1 cup dried porcini mushrooms, soaked in water
> olive oil
> 2 garlic cloves, minced
> 1 teas fresh rosemary, chopped
> 1 cup white wine
> 1/4 cup cream (optional)
> salt, pepper

Gently sauté the garlic until soft. Remove the softened mushrooms from the water, chop them and add to the pan along with the rosemary and a little salt. Save the soaking water. Sauté 5 minutes, deglaze the pan with the white wine, allowing it to reduce, then add the mushroom water, salt to taste, and continue to cook slowly until the water cooks off. At this point you can set the sauce aside to finish later. To finish the sauce, add a dusting of fresh ground pepper and the cream, simmering until the cream thickens. Toss with fresh tagliatelli, reserving a small amount of pasta water to thin the sauce as it will continue to thicken.

Sugo di Peperonata (bell pepper sauce)

This simple and versatile sauce is best made in the summer when the bell peppers are plentiful and at their peak. *Peperonata* is actually a side dish of sautéed peppers, onions and tomatoes, and this sauce is a wonderful use for the leftovers. The *peperonata* is simply pureed, some cream and butter is added and the finished sauce is wonderful over fusilli or penne, or gnocchi.

> 5 bell peppers, red and yellow, sliced
> 2 onions, sliced
> 3 garlic cloves, chopped
> 1 cup chopped tomatoes, fresh or canned
> 1/2 cup olive oil
> 1/4 cup cream
> 2 tbsp butter
> 1 tbsp parsley, chopped
> 1 tbsp basil, chopped

Sauté the peppers, garlic and onions in olive oil until soft and well cooked, then add the tomatoes and parsley. Salt to taste and cook an additional 20 minutes. Using a hand-held immersion blender, puree the mixture until smooth, adding a small amount of water or stock if it's too thick. Add cream, basil and butter and toss with the cooked pasta, using a small amount of pasta water to thin out the sauce if necessary.

Ragù di Cinghiale (ragù of wild boar)

The hills to the south of Siena, the Montagnola, are overrun by wild boar and deer. Wild game is plentiful in this part area and a variety of dishes can be found on most winter menus. People come here from all over Italy to eat wild boar and during hunting season what is not eaten fresh is frozen for later consumption or made into salami and sausage. This ragù can be made with wild boar or deer, or you can substitute the more common cow.

2 lbs ground wild boar, salted
1 medium onion, chopped fine
2 stalks celery, chopped fine
2 carrots, chopped fine
3 cloves garlic, chopped fine
3 tbsp tomato paste
2 cup red wine
1/2 cup or more olive oil
2 rosemary sprigs
2 bay leaves
4 sage leaves
5 juniper berries, crushed
2 tbsp parsley
1 cup crushed tomatoes
salt and pepper to taste

Sauté the meat in a large pot with a small amount of olive oil until browned, remove the meat and set aside. Add the carrots, celery, onion and garlic to the pan and sauté in olive oil over medium heat until softened but not browned, add the tomato paste and continue to cook another 5 minutes. Return meat to pan, add salt and deglaze with red wine. Cook 5 minutes, add tomatoes, salt, pepper, and herbs and allow to simmer over low heat 3 hours, covered. Stir occasionally, being careful not to allow the bottom to stick or burn. Serve with fresh tagliatelli or papparadelle, with a sprinkling of grated parmigiano.

Ragù Bianco di Anatra o Coniglio
(white ragù of duck or rabbit)

This lovely white ragù is made with pieces of duck or rabbit and cooked for a good long while. The meat can then be shredded off the bones to be part of the sauce, or you can remove the meat pieces, serve the sauce on top of tagliatelle and serve the pieces of meat as a second course, alongside a salad or other seasonal vegetable.

> 1 duck or rabbit, cut into pieces, excess fat removed
> olive oil
> 2 celery stalks
> 1 onion
> 3 garlic cloves
> 2 bay leaves
> 1 teas fresh rosemary, minced
> 3 fresh sage leaves
> 1 teas fresh thyme
> 1 tbsp fresh parsley, chopped
> 1 cup white wine
> 2 cups broth or water
> salt
> white pepper

Brown duck or rabbit pieces in olive oil in a large pan, remove to side. Mince finely by hand or in food processor the celery, onion and garlic and sauté in pan with additional olive oil. Add fresh herbs and the meat, deglaze with white wine and allow the wine to cook off. Add broth, cover and simmer until meat is tender and falls off bone. De-bone meat pieces, adding the meat back to the sauce and simmer 2 minutes. Serve over tagliatelle or papparadelle and serve with parmigiano.

If you would like to serve the meat as a second course, instead of de-boning the pieces, remove them to a platter and keep warm. Reheat the sauce and toss with the pasta. Serve the meat with a side of vegetables or a salad.

Sugo di Pomodoro (simple tomato sauce)

        1 small onion, chopped finely
        2 garlic cloves, minced
        16 oz tomato puree or crushed tomatoes
        parsley
        basil
        salt & pepper

Sauté onion and garlic in a good amount of olive oil until soft. Add crushed or pureed tomatoes, salt and pepper. Cook 20 minutes, add chopped parsley and basil.

Sugo di Pomodoro e Basilico Fresco
(fresh tomato and basil)

You can use any type of fresh tomato for this sauce, but the roma, or plum tomatoes, are best because they tend to be meatier, with less juice and more delicate skins. This is a fresh summer dressing for pasta.

        2 cups fresh roma or plum tomatoes
        2 cloves garlic
        olive oil
        2 tbsp fresh basil, chopped or torn
        salt

Gently sauté the garlic in olive oil until soft, add chopped tomatoes and sauté five minutes, adding salt to taste. Add the chopped basil and toss with cooked pasta, topping with parmigiano before serving.

For pizza sauce, use crushed tomatoes and add a teaspoon of chopped parsley.

Tagliatelle con Asparagi

I first tasted this pasta dish in the Veneto region, north of Padua where they are famous for their white asparagus. Green asparagus is prettier on the plate, but white is sweetest if you can find it.

3 cups fresh asparagus, cut into 1" pieces
1 garlic clove, whole
3 tbsp olive oil
3 tbsp butter
1/2 lb fresh egg tagliatelle
water

Place a small amount of water in a sauté pan with the garlic clove and bring to a simmer. Add the asparagus, cover and simmer until cooked through and tender. Discard the garlic. Add the cooked tagliatelle to the pan along with the olive oil and butter and toss. Serve with parmigiano.

Sugo di Noci e Panna (walnut cream sauce)

A traditional sauce dating from the 1400's in Siena, this is an extremely easy dish to make and is very rich and creamy.

> 1/2 cup walnuts, chopped fine
> 1 1/2 cups heavy cream
> 1/2 cup parmigiano cheese
> 4 tbsp butter
> white pepper, ground
> salt

Heat the cream on top of the stove, add the walnuts, parmigiano, and butter. Salt and pepper to taste, bring to a simmer and then turn off heat. Allow to remain hot until pasta is cooked, then toss and serve with a sprinkling of more parmigiano and finely chopped parsley. Because the pasta continues to absorb liquid and will be dry, you will need to save some of the pasta water to add when you toss the pasta to loosen and liquefy the sauce.

Pomerola (vegetarian ragù)

This long-cooked vegetarian sauce 'has a wonderful complexity of flavours.

> 1/2 cup olive oil
> 1 carrots, peeled and chopped
> 1 celery stalks, chopped
> 1 medium onion, chopped
> 3 garlic cloves
> 2 tbsp tomato paste
> 16 oz tomato sauce
> 3/4 cup red wine
> 2 tbsp basil, chopped
> 2 tbsp parsley, chopped
> 1 bay leaf
> salt and pepper

Finely mince carrots, celery, onion, and garlic and sauté them in the olive oil in a large sauce pot until soft, being careful not to brown. Add the tomato paste and sauté 5 minutes. Deglaze the pan with red wine, stirring to bring up any pieces stuck to the bottom. Add the tomato sauce, parsley, bay leaf, salt and pepper, and allow to cook at least an hour, stirring occasionally. Stir in basil before tossing with pasta, serve with a sprinkling of parmigiano.

Sugo di Pomodoro & Ricotta
(tomato and ricotta sauce)

This simple and light sauce is popular during the summer as it takes little time in the kitchen and is very fresh tasting.

1 onion, chopped finely
2 garlic cloves, minced
olive oil
1 tbsp tomato paste
16 oz tomato puree
8 oz ricotta
1 tbsp parsley, chopped
1 tbsp basil, chopped
salt & pepper

Sauté onion and garlic in a good amount of olive oil until soft. Add tomato paste and sauté, then add crushed or pureed tomatoes, salt and pepper. Cook 20 minutes, remove from heat and stir in ricotta, chopped parsley and basil, and toss with cooked pasta. Top with grated parmigiano and serve.

Sugo di Zucchini (zucchini sauce)

6 zucchini, sliced or cut into 1" sticks
3 garlic cloves, minced
olive oil
1 cup cream
1 tbsp mint or basil, chopped
salt

Add olive oil and garlic to a sauté pan, place over medium heat and sauté gently until garlic is softened, being careful not to brown. Add zucchini and continue to cook until zucchini is cooked through and soft, at least 30 minutes, adding salt to taste. Before serving, add cream and simmer 5 minutes. Remove from heat and stir in mint or basil.

Save a small amount of the water you've cooked the pasta in, drain cooked pasta and toss with the sauce. The pasta will continue to absorb the liquid and if it appears dry instead of creamy, add some of the pasta water. Toss with parmigiano and serve.

Farfalle con Gorgonzola

Melted gorgonzola and sage are wonderful together and even people who don't like blue cheese like this sauce. Although in Italy the pasta would never be served with the meat course, it's a fairly common practice outside of this country and this pasta is fabulous served alongside a grilled steak!

2 tbsp butter
2 tbsp olive oil
1 medium onion, chopped
6-8 fresh sage leaves
8 oz gorgonzola cheese
1/2 cup cream
fresh ground pepper
salt to taste

Sauté the onion in the butter and olive oil until soft and translucent, add sage leaves and continue to cook gently another 2 minutes. Add the gorgonzola and cook over low heat until melted, stirring occasionally. Add cream and bring to a simmer, being careful not to boil. Season with ground pepper and check for salt; some cheese is saltier than others. Toss with a pasta that has a wide, flat surface, such as farfalle.

Bucatini all'Amatriciana

Originally from the Lazio region north of Rome, this rich sauce filled with chunks of pancetta is popular in the southern regions of Tuscany. The original recipe called for the cured cheek of the pig (*guanciale*) and grated pecorino romano cheese, which is much saltier than parmigiano. The sauce was traditionally made without tomatoes and was tossed with a little of the pasta water before serving. The following recipe is more typical of Amatriciana made in the region today.

> 1/4 cup olive oil
> 1 medium onion, chopped
> 2 garlic cloves, minced
> 1 cup pancetta, chopped
> 2 tbsp tomato paste
> 1/2 cup white wine
> 4 cups tomatoes, crushed with juices
> generous grating of pecorino romano cheese

Sauté the pancetta in a medium sauce pot, adding a small amount of the olive oil if necessary. Remove to side and sauté onion in olive oil until soft, add the garlic and continue to cook 5 minutes. Return the meat to the pan, add tomato paste, stirring to disperse and cook 5 minutes. Deglaze the pan with the wine, allow the wine to simmer until it cooks off. Add tomatoes and salt and freshly ground pepper, simmer for at least one hour. Toss with cooked penne pasta, or use the more traditional bucatini if you can find them. Serve with pecorino romano.

Fresh Pasta Dough

Following is a basic recipe for the dough for whole egg pasta, used for making homemade tagliatelli, papparadelle and all stuffed pasta shapes. Use one egg for every two people, approximately.

> 3/4 cup all purpose flour
> 1 egg

Place flour in a bowl or on the board or table, make a well in the center, add the eggs and beat with a fork or your fingers, mixing the yolk and white together and gradually incorporating the flour. When the dough starts to come together, form it into a ball, gathering and scraping up all the lose ends of dough. Knead it until it's smooth and elastic. If the dough is at all sticky, add additional flour. The dough should be smooth, dry and becomes rather stiff the more you work with it. Depending on the humidity and the size of the eggs, you may need more or less flour, which can be determined while you work it. Cover the ball with plastic wrap and let it rest at least 10 minutes.

Use a pasta machine to elongate and shape the sheets of pasta, which can be cut into narrow or wide strips for tagliatelli and papparadelle, or used for lasagne, ravioli, or other stuffed pasta shapes.

Stuffed Pastas

Stuffed pasta originated in the north of Italy and was especially common in Emilia-Romagna, considered by many to be the gourmet center of Italy. This region to the north of Tuscany is geographically close enough to have shared the tradition with its southern neighbour for many generations. There are a number of different names for stuffed pasta shapes: ravioli, tortellini or tortelloni, cappelletti or cappellini, and agnolotti, to name a few. The two most common in Tuscany are ravioli and tortelloni and I have read that ravioli was traditionally filled with ricotta cheese, while tortellini was meat-filled.

Ravioli is simple to make, even for the novice. Take a square or round of pasta, place a small amount of filling in the center, lightly moisten the edges of the dough with a small amount of water, and then fold the pasta over the filling, sealing the filling inside. Place each finished shape to rest on a sprinkling of semolina flour or cornmeal until ready to cook, without covering. Bring a pot of salted water to boil and cook the ravioli for one minute, scoop out with a large slotted spoon or mesh strainer, immediately dress with intended sauce and serve.

Following are several recipes for fillings and sauces.

Salvia & Burro (sage and butter sauce)

4 tbsp butter (if unsalted, add a
little salt to taste)
fresh sage leaves, two per person

    Melt the butter with the sage leaves, and allow to sit for a few minutes together to meld the flavours. Reheat before serving. For a somewhat nutty flavour, you can simmer the butter with the sage until the sage leaves turn crisp. Dress the ravioli with the butter, top with parmigiano and serve. The sage leaves are eaten as well.

Sugo di Radicchio & Scamorza
(radicchio and smoked mozzarella sauce)

I learned this sauce from Chef Marco Coradeschi, owner of one of my favourite restaurants in Siena, the "Osteria del Gatto" inside Porta San Marco. Marco is an inventive chef and this delicious and evocative sauce that he serves with spinach ravioli really knocked me out! Try it with either the ricotta-herb filling or the ricotta-chestnut filling, or a plain egg pasta.

Scamorza is a type of mozzarella, which can be substituted.

> 1 small head red radicchio, sliced
> 1/2 cup smoked scamorza or mozzarella,
>   thinly sliced
> 2 tbsp olive oil
> salt

In a non-stick pan, heat the oil and gently sauté the radicchio, salting to taste, until it's cooked through and wilted. Lay the sliced scamorza on top of the radicchio, with space around the slices so they don't melt together. Take the pan off the heat, cover and allow it to sit while the cheese melts. When the ravioli are cooked, toss them on top of the sauce, wait one minute for the cheese to adhere to the ravioli, and turn them out onto your serving platter or bowls.

Ricotta & Erbe (ricotta and herb filling)

2 cups ricotta cheese
1 egg
1 tbsp basil, chopped
1 tbsp parsley, chopped
1-2 tbsp bread crumbs, as needed
1/2 cup parmigiano
grating of nutmeg
salt & pepper

Mix all ingredients together in a bowl. Depending on the wetness of the ricotta cheese, add breadcrumbs to absorb excess liquid as needed. Serve with sage and butter sauce.

Spinach can be added to this stuffing, which is most common in Siena. Take 1 cup cooked spinach, remove any moisture by twisting and squeezing the ball in a lint-free kitchen towel, chop finely and add it to the ricotta.

Ricotta con Castagna
(ricotta and chestnut filling)

20 chestnuts
2 cups ricotta, drained
1 egg
1 teas parsley
1-2 tbsp breadcrumbs, as needed
1/4 cup parmigiano
grating of nutmeg
salt & pepper

Boil the chestnuts in water for 20 minutes, or until soft. While they are still hot, peel them, removing all the brown paper like skin under the shell. If they cool off and become difficult to peel, reheat them in boiling water. Chop finely.

Mix all ingredients together in a bowl. Depending on how wet the ricotta is will depend on the amount of breadcrumbs you use. Dress with the radicchio scamorza sauce, or sage and butter.

Funghi e Tre Formaggi
(mushroom and three cheese filling)

2 cups mushrooms, finely chopped
(button, portabello, crimini)
1/4 cup dried porcini, soaked in water
1 clove garlic
1/2 cup parmigiano, grated
1/2 cup gorgonzola
3/4 cup ricotta
1/2 teas ground nutmeg
1-2 tbsp breadcrumbs
2 tbsp olive oil
salt and pepper

Sauté mushrooms and chopped garlic in olive oil until soft. Remove the porcini from the water, finely chop and sauté together with the rest. When they are well cooked, but not browned, place in a bowl and mix together with other ingredients, add a tablespoon of bread crumbs if mushrooms give off too much water to obtain a fairly dry mixture, salt & pepper to taste. Serve with Butter and Sage sauce and top with fresh parmigiano.

Zucca Gialla (winter squash filling)

2 cups butternut or acorn squash
1/2 cup parmigiano cheese, grated
1 egg
1/2 teas ground nutmeg
1/2 teas salt
pepper
bread crumbs, finely ground

Bake the squash in a 350° oven until soft. Let cool, scoop it out and mash it with a fork in a bowl until smooth, place it in a lint-free kitchen towel and wring out any excess liquid. Add remaining ingredients, adding as much bread crumbs as necessary to absorb any additional liquid from the squash. This will vary depending on the freshness of the vegetable. Mix together well. Top with either the Butter and Sage sauce or the Porcini Mushroom sauce, omitting the cream and lightening the sauce with a little pasta water.

In the town of Mantua in Emiglia-Romagna, they add ground amaretto cookies for a regional specialty.

Contorni e Verdure

Vegetables play an important part in the Italian diet and a wide variety are available all year round. Most of the vegetables we most relate to Italian cuisine weren't introduced into their gardens and cuisine until well after the New World was discovered. It's difficult to imagine what the Italian diet consisted of before the addition of tomatoes, potatoes, peppers, corn, beans and squash from the Americas.

During the winter the garden is resting and not producing a wide variety of vegetables, but still there are leeks, fennel, cauliflower, cabbages, winter greens in abundance, cardoons and a variety of cool-weather lettuces. Spring ushers in warmer breezes and the market stalls overflow with artichokes of all sizes, asparagus, piles of fresh fava beans and peas. The summer is the most colourful and the vegetables that we most identify with Italy abound. There are plump bell peppers, tomatoes, eggplant, green beans, zucchini and zucchini blossoms. The fall is my favourite time of year with wild mushrooms and porcini, winter squash and chestnuts enlivening and warming the menu.

Tuscans are known as *mangiafagioli*, or "beaneaters", and beans can be found either fresh or dried at any time of year. The most common are the cannellini, ceci, fava and borlotti, and there are some heirloom varieties, such as cicerchie, finding their way back to market. The beautiful burgundy and cream borlotti are found fresh in the markets during the summer months, but are dried for use all year round. The new fava, or broad beans, are eaten raw in the spring along with a fresh piece of pecorino cheese, a perfect culinary match. If you order this for a starter in a traditional trattoria, a pile of fava bean pods will be plunked down in the middle of your table, along with a chunk of pecorino, and you are left to happily peel away, eating the beans and leaving the empty pods in the middle of the table.

Vegetables are used in all aspects of Italian cuisine, whether at the root of a sauce, in a risotto or stew, alongside a meat dish, or raw in a salad. In the Siena area, I am reluctant to divulge, vegetables frequently are over-cooked and over-salted, and then topped with besciamella sauce and baked in the oven. My recipes have been slightly modified and lightened.

At all times of the year, the salads are fresh and filled with rucola, radicchio and baby lettuces and brought to the table with a side of red wine vinegar and good local olive oil for you to dress as you like.

Fagioli all'Uccelletto

This cannellini bean dish is found on almost every menu I've ever seen in this area. The name means "beans like little birds" because traditionally small songbirds were cooked with sage and tomatoes in the same manner. Serve with Italian sausage or grilled meats.

> 4 cups cannellini beans, soaked in
>   water at least 4 hours
> 2 bay leaves
> 1/4 cup olive oil
> 3 garlic cloves, chopped
> 1 cup tomatoes, chopped or crushed
> 8 sage leaves
> salt & pepper

Pour the soaking liquid off the beans, add fresh water to cover and bring to a boil. Skim the top of any foam that rises as the beans begin to cook. When the foam subsides, reduce to a simmer and add the bay leaves and 1 tablespoon salt, cover and cook until tender, adding more water as necessary.

Sauté the garlic briefly in a small amount of the olive oil, add the tomatoes and sage, sauté 5 minutes. With a slotted spoon, take the beans out of their cooking liquid and add to the tomatoes. Salt & pepper as necessary, cook 15 minutes to meld flavours and serve with additional olive oil drizzled on top.

Carciofi con Limone (artichokes with lemon)

While artichokes can be intimidating and prickly, they are really very easy to clean and should be used more often in America than they are. Cultivated by Italian immigrants who couldn't imagine a spring without them, they grow abundantly in California and are available in most areas. There are many varieties of artichokes grown in Italy, and in the spring it's not unusual to find five or six different kinds at the market. Just two examples are the *morelli* from Tuscany, which have little or no choke and are eaten raw in a salad; and the *mammola* which come from Rome and are the large globe chokes most frequently found in stores in America and are wonderful stuffed. Try to find small or medium artichokes for this dish.

fresh artichokes, 1-2 per person
olive oil
garlic cloves, chopped
juice from 1 lemon
salt

Sauté olive oil with garlic cloves until softened, add quartered artichokes and stir to coat with oil. Add lemon juice, salt and a small amount of water, cover and sauté until softened and done, about 15-30 minutes, depending on their size. If there is still water in the pan, remove cover and allow it to cook off. Serve with roasted chicken, grilled meats or as an antipasto.

Cleaning Artichokes: slice 1" off the top, remove tough outer leaves; depending on the size of the artichoke, this can be many layers. Peel and trim stem; the stem is edible so don't throw it away. Cut in half lengthwise and scrape out any hairy choke. Put cleaned artichokes in water with juice of a lemon to stop them from browning. Quarter the artichokes when ready to cook.

Cipolle Agrodolce (baked sweet & sour onions)

These are incredibly good and easy, the perfect side dish for barbeque or roasted meats.

4 onions (or one per person)
1/4 cup water
4 tbsp olive oil
1 teas salt
2 teas sugar
3 tbsp balsamic vinegar

Clean onions, leaving the root end in tact so the layers hold together and cut them in half. Mix the remaining ingredients together and toss with the onions, place them in a baking dish and bake at 350° for 40 minutes or until done. Turn them occasionally to coat with the pan juices and add additional water as necessary to prevent the bottom from drying out and burning. Serve warm with a mixed grill. Can also be kept in the refrigerator for several days and served cold with a mixed antipasto platter.

Patate Arrosto (roasted potatoes)

The traditional accompaniment to roasted meats, this dish uses the two most commonly used herbs in Tuscany: sage and rosemary.

6 large potatoes, peeled and cut into
    medium pieces
1/2 cup extra virgin olive oil
1 tbsp fresh rosemary, chopped fine
1 tbsp fresh sage, chopped fine
3 garlic cloves, chopped fine
2 teas salt

Mix sage, rosemary, garlic, salt and olive oil together in a small bowl. In a large baking dish, mix with potatoes and bake at 375° until potatoes are nicely browned, about 45 min to 1 hour.

Sformato (vegetable flan)

This dish is similar to a crustless quiche with more vegetable and less egg and is served as a vegetable side dish. It can be made in a baking dish or baked in little individual forms, which are then turned out and served. Many different vegetables such as broccoli or zucchini can be used, but my favorites are the winter greens.

1 large bunch of greens (kale, swiss chard)
    cooked down to two cups
2 garlic cloves, minced
1/4 cup olive oil
1 small onion, sautéed
1 cup besciamella sauce
3 eggs
2 cups milk or cream
1/2 cup grated parmigiano
salt, pepper, nutmeg
breadcrumbs

Wash and chop the greens. Heat the olive oil in a large pan, sauté the garlic briefly, add the greens and toss to coat with oil. Cover and cook over medium heat until soft, 15 minutes. Or the greens can be boiled in salted water until cooked, drained and chopped.

Beat the eggs in a large bowl, combine with milk, besciamella, parmigiano, salt, pepper and nutmeg. Stir in the cooked greens and onions, pour into a baking dish that has been buttered and dusted with breadcrumbs and top with a light coating of breadcrumbs. Bake at 350° until firm and brown on the edges. Let the sformato sit for 10 minutes before slicing or turning out and serving.

Sautéed Finocchio (fennel)

> 2 fennel bulbs, sliced
> 1 tbsp butter
> salt
> water

Melt the butter in a sauté pan, add the fennel slices, tossing to coat with the butter and sauté. Salt to taste and add a 1/2 cup of water, cover and simmer until the water has cooked off and the fennel is cooked through. Serve as is or sprinkle with parmigiano. It is also customary in Tuscany to top it with besciamella sauce and put it in the oven for 10 minutes, but that's overkill.

Zucchini con Menta (zucchini with mint)

A lovely, quick side dish when zucchini are plentiful in the summer.

> 4 zucchini, sliced (one per person)
> 2 garlic cloves, halved
> olive oil
> 1 teas fresh mint, chopped
> salt & pepper

Heat oil and garlic together in a large sauté pan. Add the zucchini, tossing to coat with oil and sauté. Add enough water to cover the bottom of the pan, add salt, cover and allow it to cook until the zucchini are just cooked through. Toss with the mint and serve. Basil also goes well with the zucchini if mint is unavailable.

Panzanella (Tuscan bread salad)

A light and flavorful summer salad that makes use of stale bread, panzanella can be served as an antipasto along with sliced salami, or as a side dish to the main course.

1/2 loaf hard, stale bread
1 tbsp red wine vinegar
water
1 cucumber, diced
1/2 red onion, diced
2 cups tomatoes, diced
1/2 cup extra virgin olive oil
2 tbsp fresh basil, chopped
1 tbsp fresh parsley, chopped
salt and pepper

Dissolve in a large bowl of water a tablespoon of salt and the vinegar. Add the bread and allow it to soak until the bread has softened. Time will vary depending on the density of the bread and how stale it is. Picking up the loaf in pieces, squeeze out as much water as possible and crumble it into a separate bowl. The bread should be spongy, not gummy or doughy.

Toss the bread with the remaining ingredients, being very generous with a good quality extra virgin olive oil, salt and pepper to taste.

Insalata di Farro (spelt salad)

Farro is an ancient grain, similar to wheat or barley, which was used extensively by the Etruscans and Romans. In America it has a close cousin in spelt, which can be substituted.

> 2 cups farro, or spelt
> 1/2 cup chopped green olives
> 1 cup canned artichoke hearts, chopped
> 1 cup cherry tomatoes, halved
> 1/2 red onion, sliced thinly
> 2 tbsp fresh basil
> 2 tbsp fresh parsley
> extra virgin olive oil
> salt, pepper

Rinse farro several times until water runs clear, place in a pot, cover with fresh water and bring to a boil, skimming off and discarding any foam that rises to the surface. Add 1 teaspoon salt, reduce heat and cook grain until it has softened, about 30 minutes. Watch the pot and add additional water as needed, keeping the grains covered.

Drain the farro and rinse with cold water in a colander to cool, draining well. Place in a large bowl and add all other ingredients, being especially generous with the olive oil. Add additional salt, stirring and tasting, and a light grind of pepper.

Zucchini Pancakes

My mother always had a large vegetable garden when we were growing up, and as the summer waxed and there was an overabundance of zucchini, this delicious side dish was at almost every meal. It is a wonderful summer side dish or a meal in itself.

3 cups zucchini, grated
4 scallions, chopped
3 eggs
4 tbsp parmigiano, grated
1 tbsp fresh basil, chopped
1 tbsp fresh parsley, chopped
2 tbsp flour
salt & pepper

Place the zucchini in a lint-free kitchen towel and squeeze to remove excess water. Combine all ingredients in a bowl, adjusting the flour and egg to the water content of the zucchini. The mix should not be wet and there should be just enough egg to hold it together. Heat olive oil in a sauté pan until hot; add a scoop of zucchini batter, spreading the batter out to form a pancake. When the pancake is browned on the bottom, turn and brown the other side. Serve with a dusting of parmigiano.

You can also bake the whole thing in an oiled cake pan, removing it from the oven when it is browned and set.

Peperonata (stewed peppers)

This satisfying summer dish is perfect with grilled and roasted meats. Whatever is leftover can be pureed on used as a sauce for pasta or gnocchi (see pasta section). I use a mix of red, yellow and green peppers for color, but never just green peppers as they tend to be bitter.

    4 bell peppers, sliced
    1 large onion, sliced
    3 garlic cloves, chopped
    1 cup chopped tomatoes, fresh or canned
    1/2 cup olive oil
    1 tbsp parsley, chopped
    salt

Sauté the peppers, garlic and onions in olive oil until soft and well cooked, then add the tomatoes and parsley. Salt to taste and cook an additional 20 minutes. Serve as a side to grilled sausages or meats. See pasta section for use of leftovers as a sauce.

Fagiolini con Dragoncello
(green beans with tarragon)

Strangely enough, although tarragon is a French herb from Provence with origins in Russia, the Siena area is the only area in Italy that makes use of it, and has been doing so since the middle ages.

green beans
1 garlic clove, whole
olive oil
fresh or dried tarragon
salt & pepper

Place the garlic clove, beans, tarragon and salt in a sauté pan and bring to a simmer over a medium heat, covering to allow the beans to steam. Cook until the beans are done to your liking, adding a small amount of water if the pan becomes dry. Remove from heat, dress with 1-2 tbsp extra virgin olive oil, and toss.

Secondi Piatti

Tuscans are famous for their grilled and roasted meats, but also have a great many meat and vegetable stews and braised dishes.

Grigliata (mixed grill)

Grilled meats have always played an important role on the Tuscan table. The old farmhouses all had huge fireplaces in the kitchen where all the cooking was done, and what could be simpler than to scrape some coals to the front of the fireplace and toss some sausages, pork steaks or lamb ribs on a grill over the hot coals. Grigliata, or mixed grill, is a common second course in this rural part of Tuscany, and you know you've found the perfect restaurant for eating grigliata when you spy the pile of wood outside the door and see the huge roaring fire banked in the kitchen for just this purpose.

A typical mixed grill will include pork T-bone steak, chicken, lamb ribs, sausages, pork ribs, and fresh pancetta slices.

A popular regional specialty originating in Florence is the "bistecca alla fiorentina", a thick porterhouse or T-bone cut of beef from the Chianina cow. Culinary simplicity at its finest, the steak is grilled over the coals from an open wood fire, then sprinkled with salt and pepper and drizzled with extra virgin olive oil and a little lemon juice. It is always served rare, *al sangue*, and two or three beefy fingers thick. Although you can order it well-done and they won't refuse you, both the quality of the meat and its taste suffer. Better to order something else.

Pollo al'Inferno (chicken from Hell!)

1 whole chicken, butterflied
olive oil
peperoncino, or cayenne pepper
salt

Rub the chicken with olive oil, salt it all over and then pepper it with the cayenne. Grill it over hot coals, turning frequently to allow it to cook evenly without burning. When it's done, cut it into pieces and serve with fresh lemons.

Maiale Arrosto con Finocchio
(roast pork with fennel)

Fennel is a common Tuscan herb and grows wild in the fields and alongside the road. The wild fennel varies from cultivated fennel in that there is no edible bulb, but the stems, fronds and seeds are used to flavour a number of pork products and dishes. Pork and fennel marry exceptionally well together, which is why they use the seeds in many fresh pork sausages. The traditional *finocchiona* is a cured pork salami made in Tuscany.

Fennel seed is also used in many cultures to aid digestion; try chewing on some fennel seeds the next time you have indigestion or have overeaten.

> pork roast
> salt
> pepper
> 2 tbsp fennel seed, ground or whole
> olive oil
> 3 garlic cloves
> 1 cup fresh fennel, chopped
> 1 cup white wine

Salt and pepper the roast. In a heavy sauté pan, heat a small amount of oil and brown the meat over a high heat, turning to brown all sides. Remove and place it in a roasting pan. Toss fresh fennel with salt and olive oil, rub fennel seeds generously onto the pork, add garlic cloves to bottom of pan along with the fresh fennel and a cup of white wine. Roast it in the oven at 400° until internal temperature reads 150°. (A digital thermometer is indispensable for this.) Remove from oven and let it rest 15 minutes before slicing. Slice the roast and serve it on a platter surrounded by the roasted fennel and topped with pan juices.

Pollo Arrosto con Erbe Toscane
(roasted chicken with Tuscan herbs)

The Tuscans use rosemary and sage constantly in the kitchen to roast and flavour most all of their meats. You will find the combination of garlic, rosemary and sage to be equally as good with roasted lamb, beef and pork. This dish is both delicious and extremely simple to make, the perfect comfort food for a cold winter night, or chilled for a summer picnic *al fresco*.

> 1 chicken
> 1 tbsp each fresh rosemary, sage,
>   and garlic, finely chopped
> 2 tbsp olive oil
> 1 lemon, sliced
> 1/2 cup white wine
> salt

Mix herbs, garlic, olive oil and salt together in small bowl. Rinse and dry chicken and place in a roasting pan. Rub herb mixture all over bird, inside and out. Place lemon slices in and around chicken, pour white wine in bottom of pan and roast until done, basting the bird with the pan juices while it cooks. Serve with roasted potatoes.

Coniglio Arrosto (roasted rabbit)

Rabbit, cut into pieces
olive oil
2 tbsp each chopped sage, rosemary
3-4 garlic cloves, halved
bay leaves
white wine

Salt and pepper the rabbit pieces, place in a roasting pan and rub each piece with the olive oil, sage and rosemary. Add garlic and bay leaves to the pan and enough wine to cover the bottom. Roast in the oven for 1 1/2 hours at 350°.

Guanciale Brasato (braised veal cheeks)

Veal cheeks, slowly braised in red wine, have a texture like velvet and are truly luscious. Ask your local butcher to order them for you.

veal cheeks, one for two-three people
olive oil
1 onion, chopped
1 carrot, chopped
1 celery stalk, chopped
3 garlic cloves, chopped
2 tbsp tomato concentrate, or 1/2 cup tomato puree
3 cups Chianti, or heavy-bodied red wine
2 bay leaves
1 tbsp each: parsley, thyme, sage, and
    rosemary, fresh & chopped
water or stock
salt & pepper

Salt the meat and brown well in olive oil in a wide, deep skillet or Dutch oven. Remove to the side, add the chopped vegetables and garlic to the pan, along with additional olive oil. Sauté until softened, about 15 minutes. Add the tomato, sauté five minutes and then add back in the meat, the wine and the herbs. Simmer 10 minutes, add 1 cup of water or stock, salt and a fresh grind of pepper, cover and continue to cook at a low simmer until the meat is tender and the liquid has reduced, at least 3 hours. Do not allow all the liquid to cook off, but add additional water as needed. Remove the meat and if there is a lot of liquid, reduce it over a high heat until thickened.

Slice the meat and serve it with the reduced sauce on top, or toss the sauce with fresh tagliatelle for a first course, and serve the meat as a second course along with a side of vegetables.

Pollo con Carciofi (chicken with artichokes)

          1 chicken, whole or cut into pieces
          artichokes, one per person
          1 orange, sliced
          1 lemon, sliced
          olive oil
          3 garlic cloves, sliced
          4 sprigs parsley
          1/2 cup white wine
          salt & pepper

Rinse and pat dry chicken and place in roasting pan. Salt and pepper all over or each piece.

Clean artichokes: cut 1" off tops of artichokes, remove tough outer leaves and peel stems. Cut into quarters, removing any choke from inside, and place in a bowl of water to which you've added juice from 1 lemon. When all artichokes have been cleaned, drain the water and toss with a good amount of olive oil, the garlic and the citrus slices, along with any juice you can catch while slicing them. Arrange the artichokes and citrus around the chicken in the pan and pour the juices over the chicken. Pour the wine into the bottom of the pan and roast at 375° until browned and done, basting with pan juices while it cooks. If using a whole chicken, cut the chicken into pieces and serve surrounded by the artichokes with the pan juices poured over top.

Petti di Pollo al Vino Bianco
(baked chicken breasts w/ white wine)

An excellent light dish for summer, this is also good at room temperature and goes beautifully with peperonata.

> 3 chicken breasts, boneless and skinless
>   (or veal cutlets)
> 6 cloves garlic, whole
> 8 sage leaves
> 1/4 cup olive oil
> 4 tbsp butter, cut into pieces
> flour
> 1 cup white wine
> salt & pepper

Slice each breast in half horizontally and pound evenly. Salt & pepper each piece and dredge lightly in flour.

Place olive oil, butter, sage leaves and garlic evenly in a baking dish, layer the chicken cutlets on top and bake in the oven at 400°. Cook 15 minutes, then turn each piece. Add white wine and continue to bake for another 20-25 minutes until the chicken is lightly browned and the wine has cooked down and forms a sauce. Serve the chicken with the sauce spooned on top.

Torta Rustica (rustic vegetable pie)

Torta rustica is a simple, rustic vegetarian second course, similar to a vegetable quiche. Instead of fluting the pastry edges, the edges are left to hang over the side of the pie pan while you fill it, then folded up and laid over the outside two inches of the pie. This gives it a rustic look. Use any combination of vegetables you like.

    pate brisee or pie crust
    any combination of vegetables:
    onion, sliced and sautéed
    zucchini, sliced and blanched
    mushrooms, sliced and sautéed
    bell peppers, roasted or sautéed
    kale or spinach, steamed or sautéed
    Filling: 5 eggs, beaten with:
    1 1/2 cup milk or cream
    1 tbsp fresh parsley, chopped
    salt & pepper
    grating of nutmeg
    1/2 cup parmigiano

Roll out the pastry dough for an 8" springform pan, leaving several inches of dough around the edges to extend up and out the side of the pan while assembling the torta. Layer the vegetables with the parmigiano in the pan and pour the egg filling over the top, then take the piecrust edges that extend over the side and fold them onto the top of the torta. They should come about halfway over the surface of the torta. This is what gives it the rustic look. Brush the pastry with a little egg wash and sprinkle with parmigiano. Bake at 350° until browned and set, about 45 minutes.

Faroana (guinea hen) con Vin Santo

Guinea hens are plentiful in Tuscany and most people who keep chickens also keep a few faroane. This dish is also excellent with chicken, duck or pheasant.

Vin Santo is the dessert wine of Tuscany and tastes a bit like a sweet sherry. If you can't find Vin Santo, use a combination of white wine and semi-sweet sherry.

> 1 faroana, cut into pieces (or chicken)
> 1 carrot, chopped
> 1 celery stalk, chopped
> 1 onion, chopped
> 2 garlic cloves
> 1 tbsp tomato concentrate or paste
> 1/2 cup tomato puree
> 1/2 cup olive oil, extra virgin
> 1-2 cups Vin Santo
> 1 bay leaf
> 4 sage leaves
> 1 stalk rosemary

Chop finely, or process in a food processor until fine, the carrot, celery, onion, and garlic. Salt and pepper the faroana pieces, heat olive oil in a pot or Dutch oven large enough to accommodate all of the pieces, and brown the fowl. Remove the faroana pieces to the side. In the same pan, add the vegetables and sauté until soft, adding additional olive oil if necessary; add the tomato paste and cook 5 minutes. Add the faroana, the herbs and the Vin Santo, scraping the bottom to deglaze the pan. Add a small amount of water or broth, cover and allow to simmer for 1-2 hours until the meat is tender, stirring occasionally to rearrange and evenly coat the pieces. (Chicken won't take as long to cook, but guinea hen and game birds take more time.) Taste for salt, adding additional if necessary. Serve topped with the pan juices.

Quaglia con Uva (quail with grapes)

I originally made this dish for a special *vendemmia* luncheon during the grape harvest, thrown by a friend for some local winemakers, and it has become my favourite fall dish. The small, dark, sweet Sangiovese grapes that are used for Chianti and Brunello wine are best for this dish.

Another small sweet fruit can be substituted, such as wild strawberries, blackberries, or fresh currants.

        4 quail, one per person
        2 shallots
        olive oil
        2 cups small, sweet grapes, red or black
        2 cup red wine, preferably Sangiovese
        4 sprigs thyme
        1 tbsp currant jelly
        salt

Use a sauté pan that can go from stovetop to oven, one without a plastic handle. Cut each quail in half, salt and pepper each piece and sauté over high heat in olive oil on each side until golden brown. Remove from pan. Sauté shallots in pan until soft, add quail and deglaze with red wine, adding thyme and grapes. Place in 400° oven for 30 minutes. Remove from oven and take quail out of pan, keeping warm on a serving platter. Return pan to stovetop and add currant jelly. Reduce juices over high heat until thick and spoon over quail. Serve with a garnish of the fruit.

Spezzatino (stew)

This is a hearty and filling winter dish and is best served over polenta. Often in Tuscany it's made with wild boar or deer, but you can use a combination of beef, veal or lamb as well.

2 lbs cubed meat, salted
1 medium onion, chopped
2 stalks celery, chopped
2 carrots, chopped
3 cloves garlic, chopped
3 tbsp tomato paste
1 bottle dry red wine
1/2 cup or more olive oil
2 rosemary sprigs
2 bay leaves
4 sage leaves
4 juniper berries (if using wild game)
2 tbsp parsley
salt & pepper to taste

Sauté the meat in a large pot in olive oil until browned, remove the meat and set aside. Add the carrot, celery, onion and garlic to the pan and sauté in olive oil over medium heat until soft but not browned, add the tomato paste & continue to cook another 5 minutes. Return meat to pan with the herbs and deglaze with red wine. Cook five minutes, add tomatoes, salt & pepper, and allow to cook over low heat 1-2 hours, covered. Stir occasionally, being careful not to allow the bottom to stick or burn, adding a little water if necessary. Serve over polenta.

Involtini di Tacchino (rolled turkey breast)

Turkey breast is common in Italy, much more so than a whole bird, and is usually sold with the two breast halves attached. One turkey breast should serve 4-6 people.

1 turkey breast, butterflied
4-6 slices prosciutto
4-6 slices fontina cheese
1 tbsp each fresh basil, sage, and parsley, chopped
3 tbsp fresh breadcrumbs
3 garlic cloves, whole
olive oil
1 cup white wine

Butterfly the turkey breast and with a mallet flatten the breast evenly. Salt & pepper both sides and lay it flat on your work surface. Mix the chopped herbs with the bread crumbs. Lay the prosciutto and cheese evenly on the turkey breast and place the herbed breadcrumbs in an even layer on that. Roll the turkey breast up, tie with kitchen twine at both ends and in the middle. Place the roll in a baking dish, rub with olive oil and place the wine and garlic in the bottom of the pan. Bake at 350° until browned and internal temperature reads 150°. Take out and let rest 10 minutes. Remove twine, slice and serve with pan juices.

Agnello Brasato con Chianti
(braised lamb with Chianti)

This dish can be made with any of the tougher cuts of beef as well, such as rump roast or shoulder.

> 2 lbs lamb roast, shanks with bone,
>   or lamb steaks
> olive oil
> 1 onion, chopped
> 1 carrot, chopped
> 1 celery stalk, chopped
> 3 garlic cloves, chopped
> 2 tbsp tomato concentrate, or 1/2 cup tomato puree
> 3 cups Chianti, or dry red wine
> 2 bay leaves
> 2 sprigs rosemary
> 1 tbsp each: parsley, thyme, sage, fresh & chopped
> water or stock
> salt & pepper

Salt the meat and brown well in olive oil in a wide, deep skillet or Dutch oven. Remove to the side, add the chopped vegetables and garlic to the pan, along with additional olive oil if necessary. Sauté until softened, about 15 minutes. Add the tomato, sauté five minutes, then add back in the meat, the wine and the herbs. Simmer 10 minutes, add 1 cup of water or stock, salt and a fresh grind of pepper, cover and continue to cook until the meat is tender and the liquid has reduced, about 2 hours. Do not allow all the liquid to cook off, but add additional water if needed.

Serve the meat with the sauce on top, or toss the sauce with fresh tagliatelle for a first course, and serve the meat as a second course along with a side of vegetables.

Bracciola (beef or veal birds)

These little rolls of meat stuffed with herbs are sometimes called *uccellini*, or "small birds".

> 8 scallopini of beef or veal, or 2 per person
> 2 tbsp each fresh parley and basil,
> 1/2 cup fresh breadcrumbs
> 1/2 cup parmigiano, grated
> olive oil
> 2 garlic cloves, halved
> red or white wine
> 1/2 cup chopped tomatoes
> salt & pepper

Mix together the herbs, breadcrumbs and parmigiano in a bowl. Pound out the meat slices until thin and even and salt and pepper them. Place them on your work surface and spread the herb mixture in an even layer. Roll them up, securing the end with a toothpick.

Heat the oil in a sauté pan and place the meat, seam-side down in the pan, browning evenly over a medium high heat. Deglaze the pan with the wine, add the tomatoes and garlic and braise over medium heat until the sauce is thickened, turning the bracciole to coat. Remove the toothpicks and serve the bracciole with the sauce spooned over the top.

Verdure dell'Estate con Salsiccia
(summer vegetables with sausage)

This hearty dish is best in the summer when every ingredient but the sausage comes fresh out of the garden. It can be served without the sausage for a filling vegetarian dinner and is excellent with a slice of good country bread spread with herb butter.

olive oil
4 cloves garlic, chopped
3 onions, chopped
4 bell peppers, red or yellow
6 zucchini or summer squash
2 medium eggplants
6 fresh tomatoes, or whole canned
2 tbsp fresh parsley, chopped
4 tbsp fresh basil
3 sprigs fresh thyme
salt & pepper
1 lb sweet or hot Italian sausage links

Wash and cut all the vegetables into large cubes. The stew will cook for up to an hour and the vegetables should be large enough to maintain their shape and not disintegrate.

In a large pot, brown the sausages and set aside. Add olive oil to the pot and sauté the onion and garlic. Add the bell peppers, stir to coat with oil and sauté 5 minutes. Follow with the zucchini and then the eggplant, salt and pepper. Add the tomatoes, parsley and thyme and allow to cook for 45 minutes or more. If the vegetables don't give up a lot of water and the stew is dry, add a small amount of water. Add salt & pepper to taste during the cooking time. Before serving, stir in the basil. You may either serve the stew with the sausages on the side or halve the sausages and reheat them in the stew. Serve with Italian or French bread and herb butter.

Herbed Butter

fresh butter
parsley, basil, chives, thyme
salt

Soften the butter and mix in the chopped herbs and salt.

Pollo con Olive e Pomodori
(chicken with olives and tomatoes)

1 chicken, cut into pieces
olive oil
1 onion, chopped
2 cloves garlic, minced
2 cups tomatoes, fresh or canned
1 cup white wine
1 sprig rosemary
1 bay leaf
1/2 - 1 cup black olives, oil cured if possible
salt and pepper

Salt the chicken pieces and brown them in olive oil in a Dutch oven or large skillet, remove from the pan and set aside. Sauté the onion and garlic in the pan, adding additional olive oil if necessary. Add the tomatoes and rosemary, sauté 5 minutes, then add the bay leaf, white wine, chicken pieces and olives. Salt and pepper to taste and cover the dish, allowing it to simmer in the liquid about an hour. If the liquid hasn't cooked off, remove the cover and allow the liuqid to reduce. Check for salt and serve.

Dolci

Cantucci (biscotti)

Known as cantucci in Tuscany, these twice-cooked almond biscotti are traditionally eaten after dinner dipped in Vin Santo.

> 3 cups flour
> 1 1/2 teas baking powder
> 1 teas salt
> zest from 1 orange or lemon
> 1 1/2 cups sugar
> 4 tbsp butter, melted and cooled
> 3 eggs
> 1 cup almonds, whole

Mix the dry ingredients together in a large mixing bowl, make a well in the center and add the butter, zest, and eggs. Beat the wet ingredients together, gradually incorporating all the dry ingredients. Pull the dough together with your hands, coating your hands with flour to avoid sticking, turn the dough onto a work surface and knead in the almonds. The dough should be rather stiff and dry, not moist and sticky. If too sticky, add a small amount of additional flour.

Divide the dough into thirds and roll each piece into a log, one to two inches in diameter, each no longer than your baking sheet. Place the logs on a greased sheet pan and bake at 350° for 30-40 minutes. The logs are done when they are medium brown in color and firm to the touch.

Remove from the oven and turn the logs out onto a board. Cut each log on a slight diagonal into individual cookies, about 1 inch wide, and return to the baking sheets. Bake an additional 20 minutes at 300° until dry.

Pere con Vino Rosso
(pears poached in red wine)

This is a lovely finish to a winter dinner party. Garnish each pear with a fresh bay leaf.

> 1 pear per person, peeled, halved and cored
> red wine
> water
> juice of one lemon
> sugar
> 2 bay leaves
> 2 cinnamon sticks
> 10 cloves
> 1 vanilla bean, or 1 teas extract
> 10 peppercorns

In a large pot put enough wine and water (2:1) to cover the pears. Add approximately 1 cup of sugar for 3 cups of liquid. Add the spices and heat to dissolve the sugar, add pears and bring to a simmer. Simmer 5 minutes, remove from heat and allow to stand until cool. Can be made up to two days in advance and kept cold in fridge. Remove pears from the poaching liquid and serve either whole or sliced with vanilla ice cream or a crème anglais sauce.

Tiramisu

This classic "pick me up", tiramisu should be made with the freshest of eggs. While you can use fresh espresso, I find that instant espresso coffee has a more intense flavour.

2 eggs
8 tbsp sugar
16 oz marscapone cheese
1 cup cream
2 packages pavesini cookies or dry ladyfingers
2 cups instant espresso coffee
1/4 cup rum or Vin Santo

Separate the egg yolks from the whites, beat the whites until stiff. In a separate bowl, whip the cream until stiff. In a third bowl, put the yolks and the marscapone and beat together with the sugar. Fold the whipped cream and egg whites into the marscapone. In a small bowl, combine the coffee and liquor.

Place a thin layer of marscapone in the bottom of a deep glass baking or serving dish. Individually dip the cookies quickly into the coffee and layer them in the pan, top with a layer of marscapone and then another layer of cookies. There should be three layers of cookies alternated with a layer of marscapone, finished with marscapone on top. Sprinkle the top with cocoa, coffee grounds or chopped chocolate and refrigerate at least 2 hours before serving.

Salame Dolce

Literally meaning "sweet salami", this traditional Sienese dessert looks just like slices of salami when it's formed into logs and sliced. It's great fun for kids to make and delicious served alongside cantucci.

1 package oro saiwa, or any
    plain vanilla cookie
3/4 cup sweet cocoa
3/4 cup unsweetened cocoa,
    preferably very dark
3 egg yolks
1 1/4 cup sugar
1 stick butter (not margarine)
2 tbsp Vin Santo or 1 tbsp rum

Keeping the cookies in their plastic package, or placing them in a plastic bag, break them into small pieces with a heavy mallet or hammer. Melt the butter with the sugar, put in a large mixing bowl and mix all other ingredients together until well combined. Mold into logs 2 inches in diameter, wrap in plastic wrap and refrigerate. To serve, slice like pieces of salami off the roll. They will keep for up to a week in the fridge.

Crostata

This is one of the most frequently made desserts in Siena. The crust tastes almost like shortbread and it resembles more a fruit cookie or jam tart than a pie, but always has the characteristic lattice top. Fresh fruit on top of the jam is optional but nice.

> 2 1/2 cups flour
> 3/4 cup butter, cold
> 3/4 cup sugar
> 2 teas baking powder
> 3 egg yolks
> 2 tbsp milk
> fruit marmalade or jam
> fresh peaches, apricots, or strawberries (optional)

Cut the butter into the flour then use your fingers to rub the butter with the flour until it forms very small pieces and is well-incorporated. Add the sugar and baking powder and mix. Form a well in the center of the dry ingredients, add the egg and milk and mix together with a fork. Form dough into a ball.

Setting a quarter of the dough aside for the latticed top, place the dough in a baking dish, pressing the dough out evenly along the bottom and 1" up the sides of the pan. The dough is too sticky to roll out and you will need to continually dust your fingers with a small amount of flour to keep them from sticking. The dough should be an even 1/4" thick. Spread a layer of jam about 1/4" thick on top of the dough, then top with fresh fruit slices if desired.

For the lattice top: taking a small piece of dough, roll into a long thin rope and lay on top of jam at a diagonal. Continue forming the lattice, attaching the edges gently to the sides of the crostata. Bake at 350° until nicely browned. Cool and cut into squares.

Crespelle with Nutella

Crepes:	Sauce:
2 1/2 cup flour	2 oranges, one sliced, one juiced
4 eggs, beaten	3 tbsp sugar
2 tbsp melted butter	2 tbsp butter
2 cups milk, more if needed	Grand Marnier, optional
2 tbsp sugar	Nutella
1/2 teas salt	

Make crepes: Mix liquid ingredients together, make a well in the flour and add the liquid ingredients to the flour. Whisk together, add salt and nutmeg. Strain the crepes batter through a fine sieve to remove any lumps.

Using a non-stick skillet or crepes pan, heat a small amount of butter or oil, add a small scoop of the batter to the heated pan, tilting and turning the pan quickly to evenly distribute the batter before it sets. The crepes should be thin and even. Turn the crepes as soon as it is cooked through, before the bottom browns. Stack them on top of each other as they are done. They won't stick together and can be kept like this for a day.

Lightly butter a baking pan. Place a teaspoon of Nutella on a crepe; fold in half, then half again so the crepe forms a triangle. Fill the baking pan and put in a 300° oven for 5 minutes.

For the sauce: melt the butter with the sugar and orange juice in a sauté pan, add the orange slices and allow to cook for 2 minutes. Add Grand Marnier if using. To serve, place two crepes on each plate, arrange two orange slices on top and pour a small amount of sauce over all. The orange slices along with the peel should be eaten as well.

Pinolata (pinenut lemon cake)

1 cup butter, melted
1 1/2 cups sugar
4 eggs
2 1/4 cups flour
1 teas baking powder
3/4 cup milk
zest from one lemon
1/2 cup pinenuts

Beat the butter and sugar together until lightened in color, add the eggs one at a time, beating after each one. Blend flour and baking powder together, add to egg mixture and mix just until wet, add milk and lemon zest and mix just until incorporated.

Stir in pinenuts and pour batter into an oiled and floured rectangular baking dish. Bake at 350° for 25-30 minutes until toothpick inserted in the center comes out clean. Place on a rack to cool. To serve, slice and top with powdered sugar and fresh strawberries or peaches.

For a simple apple cake, omit the lemon and add 1 cup chopped apples.

Pannacotta

Literally "cooked cream", this is a dessert that's easy to make and very versatile and can be served topped with fresh fruit or with a chocolate or caramel sauce. Delicious all by itself as well! Please do not substitute milk, it just doesn't work.

> 1 quart heavy cream
> 3/4 cup sugar
> 3 gelatin sheets (available at specialty
> food shops)
> 1 teas vanilla, or one vanilla bean

Soak gelatin sheets in tap water until soft. Combine cream with sugar and vanilla, in a saucepan and bring to a boil. As soon as cream begins to boil, remove from the heat, take gelatin out of water and whisk into cream. Pour into a large bowl and cool over an ice bath, stirring to release the heat. Ladle into cups or bowls and refrigerate until cold and firm, topping with a fresh fruit sauce, caramel, or chocolate *ganache* before serving.

Cappucino Pannacotta

Add two tablespoons instant espresso to the cream, omitting the vanilla, while it is heating. When it is cooled, place in coffee cups to chill. Serve the cappuccino cups on a saucer, with a dollop of whipped cream and a dusting of cocoa.

Orange-Lemon Semifreddo

For a wonderful winter dessert, take leftover slices of Christmas panettone and top them with this citrus semifreddo. It's one of the creations of my good friend Odette Fada, an excellent chef from whom I have learned countless things about food.

1 cup sugar
1 3/4 cup fresh orange & lemon juice
1/2 cup julienned zest of oranges and lemons
4 egg whites
1/4 teas vanilla
3/4 cup sugar
1 quart cream, whipped

Place the first cup of sugar together with the orange and lemon juice and bring to a boil. Add the citrus zest and allow it to boil until thickened, about 10 minutes, then take it off the heat and cool. Remove the zest with a slotted spoon and put aside.

Whip together the egg whites, vanilla and remaining sugar until stiff, then fold in the whipped cream, then the cooled syrup.

Place the semi-freddo in molds or in a baking dish and freeze until set. Serve in slices with the citrus zest on top. To top leftover panettone, place the slices in a baking dish, spread the semifreddo evenly on top and freeze until set. Slice to serve.

Mascarpone con Pesche
(peaches with mascarpone cheese)

500 grams mascarpone
3/4 cup sugar
2 tbsp cream
1 teas cinnamon
1 teas vanilla
6 fresh peaches
2 tbsp sugar
1 tbsp lemon juice

Place mascarpone in bowl, add 3/4 cup sugar, cream, cinnamon and vanilla and whip together until light. Wash and slice the peaches, tossing with 2 tablespoons of sugar and lemon juice. Distribute evenly in serving bowls and top with peaches. Plums, nectarines, or apricots can be substituted.

Cenci (little rags)

These fried strips of dough are served throughout Italy for *carnivale*, the season that preceeds Lent. Also known as *chiacchiere, stracci, lattuga,* or *struffoli* in other parts of Italy, the Tuscans call them *cenci,* or "little rags".

1 1/4 cups flour
1/2 teas baking powder
pinch of salt
1 egg
1 1/2 tbsp rum
vegetable oil for frying

Mix the flour, baking powder, salt and sugar together, add the egg and rum and mix with a fork until evenly mixed. Pull the dough together with your hands and knead until smooth.

Roll the dough until thin with a rolling pin or the pasta machine, cut into strips and fry in the oil until golden brown, being careful not to burn. Drain on paper towels and dust with powdered sugar before serving.

Schiacciatta

This sweet bread is made during the *vendemmia*, or wine harvest, in Tuscany and makes use of the small, sweet sangiovese grapes that have just been harvested.

> focaccia dough
> sangiovese grapes, washed but
>   not pipped
> extra virgin olive oil
> sugar

Divide dough into thirds, roll 1/3 out with a rolling pin to the diameter to fit the baking dish you will use. Oil baking dish well, place sheet of dough in bottom of pan. Generously sprinkle with olive oil, add grapes and lots of sugar. Roll out the second piece and place it on top of the first, following with another sprinkling of sugar, grapes and oil, continue with the final piece. Bake it in a 350° oven until browned. Cool, top with powdered sugar and serve in slices.

Bread Dough

This basic yeast dough can also be used for pizza and focaccia.

1 package dry yeast, or 1/2 cake yeast
1 1/2 cups warm water
1 teas salt
3-4 cups flour
2 tbsp olive oil

Dissolve the yeast in the water. Mix together the flour and salt in a bowl, make a well in the center and add the water and oil. Begin to stir with a fork, bringing the flour in a little at a time until all flour is incorporated. Turn out onto a floured surface and knead until smooth and elastic. Place the dough in an oiled bowl, cover with plastic wrap and set in a warm spot to rise.

Pan co'Santi (All Saint's bread)

This is a traditional round loaf made for All Saint's Day and contains raisins, walnuts and black pepper. You'll find it in the bakeries and bars during October and November and it's usually eaten for breakfast or with the fruit and cheese course as dessert.

2 3/4 cups flour
1 teas salt
1 teas black pepper
2 tbsp olive oil
1 packet active dry yeast
1/2 cup raisins
1/2 cup walnuts

Dissolve the yeast in 3/4 cup water. Mix the flour, salt and pepper together, make a well in the center and add the yeast and olive oil. Beat the wet ingredients with a fork, gradually incorporating all the flour until it forms a ball. Add the raisins and walnuts and knead on a floured surface until smooth. Place the dough in an oiled bowl, cover with plastic wrap, place it in a warm space and leave it to rise until doubled in size, 1-2 hours.

Punch the dough down, form it into a flattened round on an oiled baking sheet and allow it to rise again, about 30 minutes. Bake it at 375° until brown. It will be done when tapping on the bottom produces a hollow sound. Remove it from the oven and brush the top with a bit of beaten egg yolk. Place it on a rack to cool.

Frittelle di San Giuseppe (St. Joseph Fritters)

These fried balls of rice dough are traditionally served in honor of the feast day of St. Joseph on March 19th. Around mid-February in the Piazza di Campo in Siena, a large wooden hut is set up and frittelle are sold hot out of the oil, rolled in sugar and wrapped in a paper cone.

> 1 lb rice
> 3 quarts water
> 1 teas salt
> zest from 1 orange and 1 lemon
> 2 tbsp flour
> 1 egg
> oil for frying
> sugar for coating

Cook the rice in the salted water until the rice is really well done, stirring occasionally and adding additional water as necessary to keep the rice covered. Drain the rice, place it in a colander over a bowl and leave it to drain and dry out at least 12 hours.

Mix the rice with the citrus zest, flour and egg until it becomes fairly creamy. Heat the oil, scoop small balls of dough about 1" in diameter into the oil and fry until golden brown, turning for even cooking. Drain on paper towels and roll the balls in sugar to coat. Serve hot, warm or at room temperature.

Castagnaccio (chestnut flatbread)

This flatbread made from chestnut flour is traditionally served as a winter dessert, although there isn't any sugar in it. Chestnuts are generally considered by the Sienese to be too sweet for anything but dessert. Most chestnuts shipped to America come from the Campania region in the south, especially my Grandmother's home town of Montella, where they farm them in great quantities and are used in a number of savory dishes.

The key to this chestnut bread is good quality, fresh chestnut flour and good extra virgin olive oil.

> 2 1/2 cups chestnut flour
> 2 cups water
> 1 teas salt
> 3 tbsp extra virgin olive oil
> 1/2 cup pinenuts
> 1/2 cup raisins
> 2 tbsp rosemary leaves, whole

In a bowl add the water and oil to the flour and salt, whisking to avoid any lumps. It should be fairly liquid, about the consistency of heavy cream. Pour the batter onto a well-oiled cookie sheet with sides, or jelly roll pan; the batter shouldn't be more than 1/2 inch thick. Sprinkle the pinenuts, raisins and rosemary evenly on top, drizzle with a little more oil and bake at 350° for 40 minutes, or until it's dry and the surface cracks. Serve warm.

Bibliography, References
and Suggested Reading

"A Table in Tuscany: Classic Recipes from the Heart of Italy", Leslie Forbes, Penguin Books, 1985.

"Antipasti: the little dishes of Italy", Julia della Croce, Chronicle Books, 1993.

"The Art of Eating", MFK Fisher, Collier Books, 1990.

"Eating in Italy", Faith Heller Willinger, William Morrow and Company, 1998.

"Essentials of Classic Italian Cooking", Marcella Hazan, Alfred A. Knopf, 1985.

"Food in History", Reay Tannahill, Crown Trade Paperbacks, 1988.

"Food Lover's Companion: Comprehensive Definitions of Over 4,000 Food, Wine and Culinary Terms", Sharon Tyler Herbst, Barron's, 1995.

"The Food of Italy", Waverley Root, Vintage Books/Random House, Inc,1971.

"On Food and Cooking: The Science and Lore of the Kitchen", Harold McGee, Charles Scribner's Sons, 1984 or 2004.

"Ricettario di Siena: Testimonianze di cucina e tradizioni di un popolo", Sonia Pallai con Claudia Buracchini e Laurent Coppini, Commune di Siena, 2003.

"The Tuscan Year: life and food in an Italian village", Elizabeth Romer, Weidenfeld & Nicolson, 1984.

How to Order

Order additional copies of
Ecco la Cucina
as an ideal gift for family and friends.

Contact:

Gina Stipo
Via della Piaggetta 3
53010 Rosia (Siena) - Italy
ginastipo@yahoo.com
www.eccolacucina.com